Body and Beauty Care

Published by
Lotus Press Publishers & Distributors

Body and Beauty Care

Dr. Rajeev Sharma
B.H.M.S.; M.D. ; P.G.N.D; D.Y.Th., PMS

Lotus PRESS
4735/22, Prakash Deep Building,
Ansari Road, Daryaganj,
New Delhi - 110002

Lotus Press Publishers & Distributors
Unit No.220, 2nd Floor, 4735/22, Prakash Deep Building,
Ansari Road, Daryaganj, New Delhi- 110002
Ph:- 32903912, 23280047, 098118-38000
Email : lotuspress1984@gmail.com
Visit us : www.lotuspress.co.in

Body and Beauty Care

ISBN : 978-81-8382-256-5

Attention Readers :
Please consult to your physician before trying any medicine or treatement plan. Author/publisher will not be responsible for any reaction/loss.

***Printed & Published by* : Lotus Press Publishers & Distributors,** New Delhi- 2

Preface

This book describes well about the skin, hair and body care.

Skin is the outer covering of our body and is a very important part. A good skin and proper hair always add confidence to one's life.

In this book, besides face mask, massage, diet, makeup tips, nail and foot care, there are chapters like use of refrigerator in helping skin tone, home, ayurvedic and homoeopathic medicines for skin and hair, allergies and fungal infection,caring your hair etc.

This book conains 57 chapters and most of your skin and hair problems are discussed here with suitable treatment and corrective plans.

If anybody wants to come and consult me, first fix an appointment by phone or email and please do not come without prior appointment.

With thanks and regards,

Dr. Rajeev Sharma
AAROGYA JYOTI®
Email: drs108@gmail.com
drs108@newkamasutra.com
Visit http://www.newkamasutra.com

A Brief About

Dr. Rajeev Sharma is an eminent consultant of Homoeopathy,Yoga, Naturopathy and Alternative Medicine in India. He has written more than two hundred and fifty books (250) in Hindi and English and around one thousand articles which have been published in various newspapers and magazines. He was also an Editional Board Member of the prestigious *Asian Homoeopathic Journal* besides many other newspapers and magazines.

Dr. Rajeev Sharma has written books on ayurveda, allopathy, homoeopathy, yoga, naturopathy, accupressure, magnetotherapy, reiki, water-therapy, massage and aromatherapy etc.

The books written by Dr. Rajeev Sharma are published by renowned publishers of India. Besides this he is doing editing and translation also. He is content provider to many magazines.

Dr. Rajeev Sharma has written books on all major ailments like diabetes, hypertension, obesity, stomach and respiratory disorders, E.N.T. disorders, female disorders, UTI disorders, paediatric problems, headache, stress and other mental problems and Sexual Disorders etc. You can fix an appointment for any of such problem.

Dr. Rajeev Sharma is Medical Advisor to Ralson Remedies (a homoeopathic manufacturer), and Dixit Pharmacy (Ayurvedic Manufacturer), and Medical Officer in U.P. Govt.

He has received several prizes for his outstanding achievements. He has been awarded the *Best Author prize in Hindi* by the Ministry of Health and Family Welfare,

Government of India and *Sarjana Puraskar by U.P. Hindi Sansthan,* Lucknow. He has delivered talks on All India Radio and lectures on Alternative Medicine in various Government and Non-government Organisations. He has written Advt. Scripts for the products of several companies.

He is delivering lectures and providing literature on Yoga, Pranayama, Meditation, Stress and Life Style Management to the MNC's and corporate houses.

He has established a website through which you can get Online Training or e Books in Accupressure, Massage, Yoga, Water Therapy, Diet Therapy, Naturopathy, Colour Therapy and Reiki besides other paramedical courses.

Dr. Rajeev Sharma is also a social activist. He has worked a lot against Addiction and Prevention of AIDS.

He has worked for human rights too and has received the World Human Rights Promotion Award. His name has been published in *LIMCA BOOK OF RECORDS* and is to be published in India Book of Records 2011.

He has developed a website :-
www.newkamasutra.com : A site of love, romance and sex.

Newkamasutra is a scientific site to guide for love, romance, relationship, dating, sex related and other problems. The information given here is not porn but scientific, relevant and authentic.You can update your knowledge by viewing "Vatsyayan's Kamasutra", "Newkamasutra", "Dating and Romance", "Sex Education", "Sexual Disorders", "Aphrodisiacs and Diets", "Sex Yoga" etc.

Besides this you can do Consultationf and Online Coursesf or purchase an eBookf of your choice or shop from Storef. Forumf also provide facility to interact with viewers of our site.

We do not believe in magical remedies or untrue claims. We treat individuals on the basis of the totality of their symptoms. Thus the consultation and medicines provided are personalized.The ultimate aim of our organization is to provide quality information, medicines, teachings and techniques. This is called **QMT.**

Contents

1

Body Care

After an exhausting day your body needs to be relaxed and pampered in order to get a good night's sleep. You must take care of your body not only in the day but in the night as well. While you sleep at the night, the body is resting and replenishing itself. There are a few things that you can do to relax the body to help in the replenishing process. Here are a few ideas for bath and body care in the night:

- Take a warm, soothing bath. Fill your bathtub with warm water and some lavender that helps in calming and relaxing the body and reduces muscle tension. You can add chamomile, which is a skin soother and helps in reducing swelling and pain in the skin. Lie in the bath tub for some time and let these herbs relax your body and mind.
- If you want to wake up with a tan you can use a self-tanning lotion overnight. Exfoliate your skin with a scrub and moisturise. Once the moisturiser is fully absorbed spread the self-tanning lotion evenly all over your body, working on one portion of the body at a time. Use wipes to wipe the tanner off your

palm and fingers as you apply the lotion. Today, there are many self-tanning lotions that dry in five minutes.

- Your hands are the first to show signs of aging and often neglected as well. Give your hands a new lease of life. Apply a generous amount of rich hand cream to restore lost moisture. This is an important part of night body care.
- While sleeping in your bedensure that your neck is properly supported through out the night. Buy a good quality people to help keep the stress off your neck. Your sleep should rejuvenate you so ensure that every part of your body is taken care of properly.
- Ingrown hairs block pores and can cause bacteria to develop, resulting in redness and swelling. Use a cream that has glycolic and salicylic acid that removes the bacteria. Make it a part of your night care routine for a few nights and you will get rid of ingrown hairs.
- Your feet support the weight of your entire body. Find time to take care of them. If they are callused and cracked moisturise them well. If they are cracked use a foot cream that has glycolic acid. Apply this cream before you sleep and slip on a pair of clean cotton socks. This should be another important part of your body care routine every night.
- Light aromatic candles in your bedroom. These candles will provide a soothing atmosphere and relax your senses. Just remember to blow them out before you sleep.
- Keep the humidifier running in the bedroom to keep the air moist. Your skin will glow and be replenished by the moist air through out the night.

- Use a "hot stone massage" to heat your heart. This treatment that is common in spas can be done at home too. You need a smooth flat stone as large as the human hand. You can find one on the beach or buy one in a skin care bou-tique. Follow the instructions given below:
- Boil water in a pot.
- Add rosemary, clove and pepper-mint into the water.
- Put the rock into the water and let it stay there till it is heated.
- Put off the heat rock and allow the rock to turn nice and warm.
- Lie down in a dark or softly lit bedroom and place the warm rock between your breasts, on your chest. Allow the warmth and aroma of the stone to relax you and soothe you into a deep peaceful sleep.

Bathing

Bathing is much more than just sitting in a tub. One of the most important ways through which you take care of your body is to by having a good bath. A bath cleans and refreshes your body and is relaxing for the mind as well. It is important to have a bath everyday, in order to maintain good personal hygiene as well. Having a bath early in the morning refreshes you and makes you ready for the whole day. On the other hand, bathing in the evening or night removes all the dust, grime and sweat that you have gathered throughout the day and ensures that you are able to get a good and peaceful sleep.

There are various kinds of baths in the present day world, including private baths, public baths, Turkish baths, public swimming pools (also known as swimming baths), steam shower baths, sponge bath, hot baths and cold baths, each suiting a different need. Today, the concept of luxurious bathing has also caught on. Making the right kind of arrangements in the bathroom and adding the right kind of accessories can go a long way in making your bath not only enjoyable, refreshing and soothing, but luxurious as well. In the following lines, we have listed the best tips for luxurious bathing, which will ensure the perfect beauty and a really beautiful body for you.

Luxurious Bathing

- First of all, you need to prepare the bathroom and the bath.
- Create a soothing and peaceful environment in the bathroom.
- Light aroma candles or scented candles and play some relaxing music in the background.
- Arrange a comfortable bath pillow, which will help you relax.
- Now, turnoff the phone and switchoff the answering machine, to avoid any disturbance.
- Fill your bathtub with warm, not hot water. It will help you relax.
- Add bath salts and essential oils to your tub.
- Lie down in the tub and soak yourself for 15-20 minutes. Let your mind and body relax.
- To clean yourself, make use of a fragrant soap, along with body sponge, loofah or brush.

- Massage your skin in a circular motion.
- Rinse off your body with water.
- Pat your skin partially dry with a towel. Please do not rub.
- Immediately after drying yourself, apply your favourite moisturiser while the skin is damp. Doing so will lock in the moisture from your bath.

• • •

2

Perfumes

Both men and women use perfumes or fragrances. Everybody likes to smell nice and pleasant and nobody wants to stink of body odor. Women have a wide range of perfumes to choose from. There are perfumes specifically meant for the day and those that are specially meant for the night. Many people do not know how to buy perfumes. Here are a few points as to how to choose a perfume:

- Try the perfume before you buy it.
- Try buying new perfumes. While buying new perfumes limit yourself to three perfumes, as your nose will not be able to differentiate between the perfumes if you try too many.
- The same perfume will smell different on different people because it will react differently to each person's body.
- Wait for 10 minutes after applying the perfume, it will give you the right smell after it reacts with your skin.
- After buying the perfume of your choice you would like to get the most out of the perfume. Here are a few tips on how to get the best out of the perfume:
- Do not expose your perfume to extreme temperature and sunlight. After the perfume bottle is opened the

perfume will change and exposure to sunlight will disturb the delicate smell of the perfume. Store it in a cool dark place to keep the fragrance intact.

- Use shower gel, body lotions and body sprays of the same fragrance as your perfume it will last longer if you do this. Use your perfume as a highlight on your pulse points finally.
- Perfumes should be used throughout the day. Even concentrated perfumes do not last for the whole day. You will have to re-apply every 3-4 hours.
- Use a different perfume for the morning and a different one for the night. Choose a perfume according to your mood.

Here are some interesting facts about perfumes:

- Women have a keener sense of smell than men.
- The sense of smell is affected by your medication, diet and lifestyle.

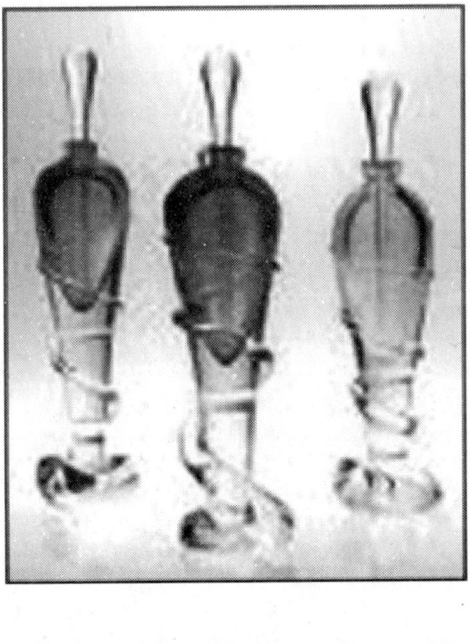

- Perfumes react differently on blondes, brunettes and redheads.
- Our ability to remember smell is greater than the ability to remember things that we have seen.
- Our sense of smell is sharper in the latter half of the day.
- The older you grow the less sharp your sense of smell is.
- Perfumes rise and if worn only on the face or behind the ears, it will rise and vanish quickly.
- Oily skin holds perfumes better than dry skin.
- Perfume once opened will fade with time.
- Increase in altitude reduces the lasting ability of a perfume.

• • •

3

The Right Way to Wash your Face

Skin Care plays quite a big role in **beauty** and keeping your image and this involves the techniques with which you use for cleaning. Washing the face is indeed a sensitive matter as this may well end the occurrence of **wrinkles**. Since wrinkles tend to strain the facial muscles, it is good to know how to stave them off when they try to form on the **face**. Numerous **skin products** have been put out in the market in recent years and it may be important to consult of an expert in the beauty market before buying any facial soap or lotions.

With many sebaceous glands being harboued under the skin of the human face, this tends to be the oiliest part of the skin. The industry has come up with a number of creams that create a protective film around the face in case of air pollutants that may affect your skin tone. Aggressive cleaning is, however, needed at the end of the day to make sure that the skin is completely free of the pollutants.

Since the **facial skin** has quite a thin outer layer, it is one of the most sensitive parts of the body thus severe scrubbing may cause the facial skin a lot of irritation. When washing the face, it will be important to choose a cleanser that is mild to the facial nerve endings. Thus you are able to take care of the residue and let your face enjoy the airiness.

When washing the face, one should not use the same soap that they use for bathing their bodies. Liquid body wash agents do not count in the practice of facial cleansing. Anyhow, facial cleansing is quite a simple process and becomes fun with perfection.

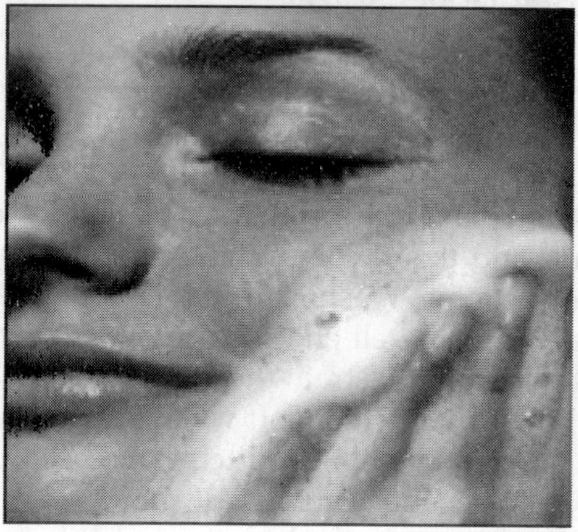

The **face needs the mildest of soaps** and sometimes it is not even necessary to use any soap on the face, which is unless you are shaving since this needs lather. Otherwise, when proceeding to the cleaning, you may need to wash your hands first before you start the proper cleaning. Without the facial soap, a face cloth comes in quite handy, worthy of note also is that it is not a good thing to wash your face with cold water. Water that has been warmed a bit makes sense for the hygiene of your skin. This wipes of the dirt from the face as much as it will soothe off the irritation on the facial nerves. The face cloth is already embedded with soap and therefore it eliminates the need for using the soap.

One may consider using new tools put out in the market in the recent past, this includes the electric toothbrush which has proved to be quite efficient in taking care of residue that may settle on the face in your daily goings-on.

Non-foam cleaners also work a whole load of wonders since they don't leave your face coated with any chemicals after use. Also remember to use your fingers to gently massage your facial muscles.

• • •

4

Types of Skin

Human skin has been divided into the following categories:

- Normal Skin
- Greasy Skin
- Dry Skin
- Sallow Skin
- Combination Skin
- Sensitive Skin
- Chapped Skin
- Withered Skin

We shall be discussed each of them separately.

Normal Skin

A clear, fine textured, supple and smooth surface which is neither greasy nor dry are some of the characteristics of this type of skin. The possessor of this skin generally keeps good health which stems from smooth blood circulation. Not requiring much of the care, even if normal body cleaning operations are performed twice a week, this type of skin maintains its healthy glow. However, remember you should not use hard soap but only mild baby soap for hard soaps with their acidic contents tend to remove-the normal shine of the skin earned by the natural and healthy flow of blood. At night, in order to keep your skin's normal moisture balance, apply a thin film of any home made moisturiser. In case, due to vagaries of weather you feel your skin getting more oily or extra-dry in any area of your body, you may apply the lotion or remedies mentioned later for these varieties of skin. But remember to treat only the particular area and not the whole region.

Greasy or Oily Skin

Normally this variety of skin has coarse pores and pimples or other embarrassing blemishes. In case you have such type of extremely oily skin, take a diet rich in proteins but restricted in sugar, fluids and salts. Also take plenty of leafy vegetables and fresh fruits. Pork and fried and highly seasoned items of food should be avoided. Have your blood brought upto par by suitable administration of necessary vitamins, iron, minerals and similar substances. Besides taking internal care of yourself, you should also take equal care of yourself externally. Half an hour before taking your bath apply on your face half teaspoon each of lime and cucumber juice mixed together. If it is excessively oily, mix a few drops of Eu-de-cologn. This not only helps keep oiliness away but also helps in opening the pores of the skin by acting as astringent, thereby preventing acne. At times your make up would appear to be becoming patchy either on the forehead, chin or more due to excessive oiliness in these areas. The best remedy, in such cases, is application of the cold cucumber juice on the excessively oily parts of your face, dry it thoroughly and then apply your make-up. In case your whole face turns patchy after make-up is applied on it, then apply equal parts of lime juice and witch-hazel. Dry before putting on your make-up. Applying cold pack, following the drying operation, will add to the lustre of your skin.

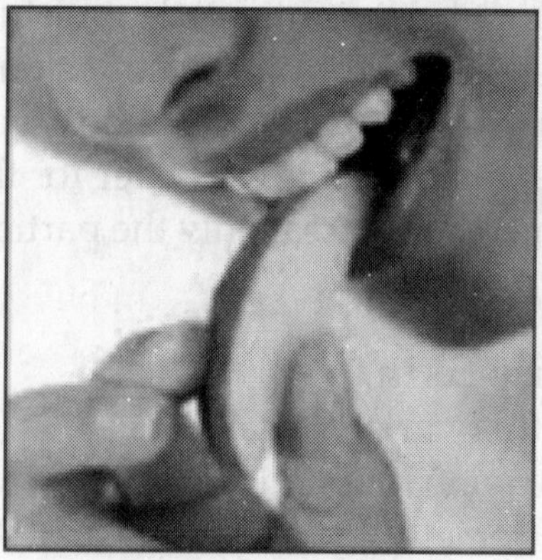

Sallow Skin

This is a typical skin with a distinct 'Colourless look'. It appears almost dead, lustreless and devoid of normal vital glow. Such persons invariably are the patients of anaemia with their diet substantially lacking in Vitamin 'B' and Iron. The Vitamin B, particularly B is very good for curing you of paleness because it keeps the skin well-nourished and rose by keeping the blood circulation normal. Also active physical exercise will help you as it keeps the blood circulation normal. Fresh blood and increased oxygen remove that dull and blemished look of the skin.

For fighting against the malady of this type of skin, there is an exercise called 'The Hollywood glam' which in face, is not a whole exercise but just position. But it helps you greatly overcome this trouble. Lie flat on your bed with your feet elevated 12 inches higher than your head. Start with 10 minutes of elevation and gradually work up to 30 minutes. The cleansing technique depends on whether your skin is dry, oily or normal. Also, if your skin is not extra-sensitive, a good idea is giving yourself a facial, once a week, to give an impetus to your blood circulation. More exercises for skin-care will be discussed later.

Combination Skin

Combination skin means the type of skin that is both oily or greasy, and dry in different parts of the body. Normally, people of this type of skin have a greasy centre panel consisting of nose, forehead and chin. Why a dry panel consisting of cheeks, mouth and the areas around the eyes? As mentioned in the skin categories of the relevant type, treat dry areas with home-made cold or moisturising creams, while greasy patches with regular home-made astringents. Some special home-made creams and whiteness recipes are given ahead.

Sensitive Skin

A sensitive skin is a thin or fine textured skin that looks very delicate. It reacts quickly to both heat and cold. It, therefore, gets sunbruns or windburns quite easily. If you have this type of skin, use sun-screen lotions or creams. Wash your face with mild baby soap, rinse thoroughly and pat the skin dry with a soft towel. Such people should never use rough towels. Also it is important for the people of this type of skin that they should never use any cream or lotion or perfume/dry etc., even synthetic clothes without first conducting their priorities of the material on the inside of your wrist to see the reaction of your skin to the substance. It is because not many items of make-up agree with a sensitive skin. Also applying home-made moisturising cream on your face before retiring for the night is a necessary precaution for the persons with sensitive skin.

Chapped Skin

The rough texture of the skin which appears to be cracking sometimes falls in this category. In case the cracks develop on your skin, then every day, at bed-times, take the white of an egg, mix in one ground almond and sharply apply on your face. When the skin feels dry, wash off the paste with water and apply home-made nourishing cream. Such persons should avoid using soap totally because due to its acidic reaction soap dissolves the fat from the skin and takes them away from the surface. Instead, clean your skin with gram flour made into paste with fresh bath, massage yourself either with warm olive, mustard or coconut oil. Also, after bathing blot yourself dry; don't rub yourself rigorously with a bath towel. Every night, before you retire, apply home-made cold-cream. In case you cherish to maintain the youthful loveliness of a clean and flawless complexion, use cold or nourishing cream every night after crossing 25 years of age. Such persons shouldn't wear tight-fitting woollens or rough clothes because they have the tendency to aggravate this itching or scaling. If you have to use woollens first wear woollens without their having any evil effect. In case you have developed scales the ideal remedy is to take saline bath. Prepare the bath in the following way: Add about 20 gms of sodium chloride (table salt or rock salt) in a tubful of water and soak in this water for about 15 to 20 minutes twice daily. Getting out of the tub, let your body dry naturally and then massage gently either with Almond or Olive Oil. Although appearing simple, this treatment often brings about a great reduction in chapping and scaling. This also provides great relief from itching. However, this treatment is recommended only when you are in the zenith of your health.

Withered Skin

This is a typical type of skin which has a very rough texture usually replete with wrinkles. It is due mainly to over-exposure to extremes of climate as too much heat or too much cold causes this state of skin. To protect yourself from falling a victim to such a skin, always use sun-screen lotions or creams whenever you have to go outdoors for a good length of time. Soap being a taboo, always clean your face with milk cream, soap tends to as aggravate the problems of this type of skin. Also, do not forget to use a moisturising cream at night. Make the mixture the following way and use it in the morning half an hour before taking bath. Take an egg's white half an hour before taking bath and mix in one tablespoon of honey and one-fourth teaspoon of carrot juice. Let this mixture remain on your skin for about 20 to 30 minutes. Don't remove it rubbing off with hands but with a cotton wool-soaked in warm water (to which a little of soda bicarbonate has been added). This treatment will surely remove roughness and wrinkles from the skin. Also, when you go to take your bath, add two tablespoons of olive oil to the water in the tub before entering it. The ladies, with this type of skin, should use moisture laden make-up base in all the seasons. Also they must not ever prefer an ordinary skin but a lipstick with a creamy base. These external precautions will keep your even withered skin glowing naturally.

Identify Your Skin Type

By answering the questions below you can find out what type of skin you have. Just tick the answer a, b, c or d that closely applies to your skin.

1. After cleansing, how does your skin feel?
   (*a*) Tight and rough
   (*b*) Smooth and supple
   (*c*) Slightly oily
   (*d*) Oily in some areas, tight in others.
2. How often does your skin breakout in spots?
   (*a*) Almost never
   (*b*) Rarely

(*c*) Often

(*d*) Only in the T-zone (across the forehead and down the nose and chin).

3. Which of the following best describes your skin texture?

(*a*) Smooth and transparent

(*b*) Firm and even

(*c*) Slightly rough and uneven

(*d*) A mixture of the above

4. How does your skin look during the day?

(*a*) Flaky and chapped

(*b*) Clean and fresh-looking

(*c*) Shiny

(*d*) Shiny in the T-zone

Now add up how many a's, b's, c's and d's you scored.

If the majority of your answers are a's, your skin is dry.

If the majority of your answers are b's, your skin is normal.

If the majority of your answers are c's, your skin is oily.

If the majority of your answers are d's, your skin is combination.

Basic Structure of your Skin

Knowing a title about the structure of your skin will help you appreciate why certain things are good for it while others are not. Understand your skin and you are half-way to a glowing, healthy complexion.

The skin consists of three main layers: the epidermis, dermis and hypodermis.

Epidermis

The epidermis is the outermost layer and is a microscopic 0.2 mm (8/1000 inch) thick on the face. The surface consists of dead cells which are in the process of flaking away and new ones which are growing to take their place. Between the epidermal cells are formed and progress to the surface. It takes approximately twenty-eight days for a new cell to reach the top.

Dermis

The dermis is usually 1.8 mm (7/1000) thick. It is composed of a fibrous protein called collagen, elastin, which make the skin supple, and a network of blood vessels, nerves, oil and sweat glands, pores and hair follicles.

Hypodermis

The hypodermis is the tissue beneath both epidermis and this dermis. It contains muscles, veins and fat-cells and its thickness varies according to the part of the bodies.

The sebum and sweat produced by the oil and sweat glands in the dermis form a hydrolipidic film on the skin. This film, known as the 'acid mantle' Iubricates the skin's surface, helps to repel bacteria and protects against irritation. The acid mantle maintains the skin's slightly acid (pH) level. It takes one to two hours for the skin to return to its normal pH level after washing. Harsh cleansers, such as soaps, reduce the removal process. It is the activity of the sebaceous (oil-producing) glands that determine your skin type.

Functions of the Skin

- Provides a protective barrier between the environment and the body.
- Shields internal organs from injury, sunlight and germs.
- Sensory organ–it is sensitive to touch, pain and temperature.

- Keeps body temperature constant.
- Provides a waterproof barrier.
- Serves to maintain the balance of body fluids.
- Organ for elimination of fluids, minerals and other biochemicals.

●●●

5

Sensitive Skin Care

This skin is delicate and difficult to look after. It is usually easily irritated, and reacts to adverse weather conditions, changes in temperature, sunshine, perfumed products, and harsh ingredients such as detergents. The resulting dryness, blotches and rosy patches require careful management. If in fact, you do have sensitive skin, you'll have to be especially careful about what products you use on your skin and how you treat it. Here's to avoid or use on sensitive skin only under a doctor's direction.

- Clensers containing alcohol, lanolin, fragrance, benzoyl peroxide, salicyclic acid, and glycolic acid
- Toners or astringents containing alcohol
- Products containing essential oils (concentrated oil extracts from plants)
- Witch hazel
- Moisturiser containing fragrance, lanolin, dye, vitamin E
- Sunscreen containing fragrance, oil, PABA
- Makeup containing oil
- Alphahydroxy acid or retinol products (Retin-A)
- Acne medications
- Bleaching creams

- Detergents and fabric softeners containing fragrance or preservatives

To protect your sensitive skin, shop for products and makeup with labels that say "alcohol free," "fragrance free," "sensitive skin," or "non-comedogenic".

Wash once or twice a day with a soap free cleanser, or super-fatted, or unscented bar to prevent sensitive skin becoming irritated and blotchy. Soap makes delicate skin more sensitive by removing oils and moisture. Super-fatted cleansers are less drying but can leave behind a residue that blocks pores. Steer clear of toners, and simply rinse off excess cleanser with warm water, or cucumber water. While washing hair in the shower, tilt your head back to avoid getting potentially irritating shampoo or conditioner on your face. Don't forget to wash your hands frequently throughout the day and try not to touch your face. Your hands will transmit to your face the residue of all types of irritating products.

Avoid harsh skin care-products like abrasive facial pads or grainy face and body scrubs, which can strip away the protective top layer of skin–your defensive armor against heat, cold, pollution, irritants and other antagonists.

If you have sensitive skin, the eyes require extra vigilance to avoid nasty reactions. "Your eyelids are so thin and so sensitive to irritants that they often become dry, scaly and itchy." So avoid using harsh soap and alcohol-based astringents and toners. Cleanse away eye makeup with an oily remover rather than oil free product. Whatever product you use, gently stroke away eye makeup with a cotton swap or pad. Scrubbing with tissue or wash-cloth can irritate your lids.

Choose a light (water-based), non-perfumed moisturisers formulated for sensitive skin. Use sunscreen during the day. Avoid products formulated with chemical sunscreen like PABA (para-aminobenzoic acid) or the cinnamate or oxybenzone families of sunscreens, all of which can irritatate sensitive skin.

Optional: Exfoliate weekly with a gel mask containing very mild ingredients, such as aloe.

• • •

6

Combination Skin Care

Begin by washing the oilier areas of forehead, nose, and chin first for one minute and then concluding dryer area for a total cleansing time of one and a half minutes. This allows more time to be removing the oil and debris that has accumulated on the forehead, nose, and chin. As with oily skin, cleanse gently. Avoid washing more than twice a day.

Consider using a light creamy cleanser, a nonsoap cleanser, or a glycerin soap, which attracts some moisture to the skin, twice a day during cooler seasons.

Use a more moisturising cleanser during the months surrounding winter because the cheek area and even the chin can become moderately dry at this time while the forehead and nose may remain slightly oily. Switch to a less emolliating cleanser products in spring and summer.

Also, since oil on the forehead and nose can come from your hair, make some adjustment in your hair-care regimen as outlined for oily skin. That is, try washing your hair at least once a week and wear it pulled or brushed back from the face. Avoid applying hair oils or pomades on the scalp near the forehead.

Apply a light moisturiser once or twice a day to the dry areas of the oily skin. You will probably not need to apply moisturiser to the forehead and nose, which are typically oily. Choose a sunscreen gel with SPF 15 or a light oil-free lotion containing sunscreen.

DO'S AND DON'T FOR COMBINATION SKIN

Do:

- Choose cleansers for combination skin; they are formulated to be gentle on dry spots, tougher on the T-zone.
- Apply products only where you need them–moisturiser only on dry areas, benzoyl peroxide products right on blemishes.
- Smooth on a sunscreen with SPF 15 or a moisturiser or foundation with built-in sunscreen protection every day.

Don't

- Use two kinds of cleanser or moisturiser on different parts of your face; seek out products formulated for combination skin.
- Use balancing lotions; they neither endow dry areas with moisture nor reduce the amount of oil your oil glands produce.
- Apply moisturiser before working out.
- Forget to wear sunscreen.

• • •

7

Tips for Maturing Skin

What you ingest affects facial muscles and supportive tissues as well as the epidermal surface. To compensate for the body's gradually slowing cell production and less efficient metabolism of foods, it is important to provide it with ample protein (meats, eggs, dairy products, legume-grain-milk combinations), and with a generous supply of vitamins.

Here are tips to enhance natural skin care as you grow older:

- Taking a daily B-complex tablet is good insurance. Laboratory tests have shown that a deficiency of any one of the B's causes young animals to develop the wrinkled aspects of old age.
- If you smoke, stop. Smoking has been shown to accelerate aging of skin, so quitting now is important for good skin health. Use a sunscreen with an SPF of 30 or more whenever you go outdoors, especially when you are participating in sports or exercise. Be sure to reapply the sunscreen every two hours.
- Vitamin C is good for collagen and elastin, the intertwining fibres supporting your face. Collagen cannot be absorbed from even the most convincingly

advertised cosmetic, it is produced and maintained by the body from ingested protein and vitamin C with the assistance of the B-complex. Taking 1,000 to 5,000 milligrams of vitamin C in divided doses each day helps preserve and rejuvenate collagen's ability to prevent lines, sags, and wrinkles.

• • •

8

How to Care for your Skin from the Inside?

What you eat, or don't eat, is revealed by your skin: nutrients absorbed into the bloodstream nourish it through loops of capillaries close to the surface. Radiantly healthy skin is one of the dividends of eating a nutritionally balanced diet, taking supplements when needed, and drinking six to eight glasses of water each day Fruit and vegetable juices or herbal teas may be substituted for some of the water. Alcoholic drinks and caffeine-containing beverages, (regular coffee, tea, some herbal teas, many soft drinks) act as mild diuretics to dehydrate your system, so they shouldn't be counted on for filling the quota.

Protein

Skin is predominantly protein, requires a daily supply from the foods you eat because protein molecules are not absorbed through the epidermis into underlying tissues, and registers a deficiency by becoming slack and loose. Collagen-containing protein foods (avocados, brewer's yeast, dried legumes, nuts, sesame and sunflower seeds, whole grain cereals) help prevent and smooth out wrinkles. Other protein foods (fish, meats, poultry, eggs, dairy products, vegetable proteins) help your body equalize the balance between new and dying cells.

Fats and Oils

The unsaturated fats in vegetable oils assist assimilation of fat-soluble vitamins A, D, and E; contribute to your own natural oils to give your skin a sheen, plump out fine lines, and create the fresh-faced look of youth. One or two tablespoons a day can be used as salad dressing or whizzed in the blender with milk, fruit, or vegetable drinks.

Fruits, Vegetables, and Fibre

In addition to varying amounts of protein and the complex carbohydrates needed for energy, fruits and vegetables provide the fibre to keep you vibrantly beautiful and healthy by flushing toxins out of your body and avoiding constipation. Fresh, raw foods also contain enzymes that act as the body's housekeepers to keep the bloodstream clear, and, cooked or uncooked, fruits and vegetables offer an appetizing supply of vitamins and minerals necessary for skin health.

Vitamins and Minerals

Overindulging in anything, particularly fat-soluble vitamins A, D, and E, can be dangerous. Some of the following supplements may be in order, however, because individual requirements may be higher than the official RDA (recommended dietary allowance), and because eating sufficient quantities of their natural food sources is either impractical (6 oranges equal 500 milligrams of vitamin C) or would lead to unwanted weight gain.

Vitamin A is used to preserve a smooth skin texture, prevent dryness, and avoid blemishes or hasten their healing.

B vitamins are vital for clear, luminous skin. Only about 1 percent of the water-soluble, must-be-replenished-daily B complex ingested is routed to the skin, and, because they function interactively, a deficiency of any of the B's can cause skin problems. Insufficiencies may make themselves apparent by inflamed fissures at the angles of the nose and mouth, scaly lips, premature wrinkles, or by other skin disturbances.

Vitamin C, in conjunction with protein, is necessary for the production of collagen—the glue that holds us and our skin together and circumvents sags or wrinkles. Combined with bioflavonoid, vitamin C helps prevent the pigment clumping that the sun turns into "age spots," and strengthens capillaries to avoid easy bruising. Vitamin C also helps the oil-secreting glands function properly to keep the skin from drying out.

Vitamin E, necessary for healthy, moist skin, is an antioxidant present in vegetable oils; yet additional amounts of E required to prevent the E in the oils from oxidation within body. Biochemical research has demonstrated that large doses of vitamin E double healthy cell reproduction to slow the aging process and forestall premature wrinkling.

Minerals all contribute to our beauty and well-being. Two of the most essential for skin care are:

Copper

It is important for the production of skin pigment and for the prevention of blotches under the skin from ruptured blood vessels. It also cooperates with other nutrients to preserve the integrity of the elastic-like fibres supporting the skin.

Zinc

Aids in the formation of collagen, helps prevent dry skin and stretch marks, and promotes blemish healing. Without enough zinc a deficiency of Vitamin A can occur even though the intake of that vitamin appears adequate.

• • •

9

How to Care for your Skin from the Outside?

If you treat your skin with tenderness, it will respond with finely textured dewy freshness. If you neglect your skin, overexpose it to the sun, abuse it with harsh soaps and abrasive cleansers, irritate it with stinging astringents, or suffocate it with leftover makeup and heavy creams, it will retaliate by flaking away, erupting in bumps, developing splotches, bursting its capillaries, and wrinkling prematurely. Caring for your skin gently and consistently is the key to extending its youthful appearance.

Skin's response to a programme of systematic care is almost instantaneous, and, as young cells migrate up through the dermis to replace dead cells sloughed off the surface in a constant process of self-renewal, we have a "new" face every 28 days. "Regimen" sounds intimidating. A daily routine of skin care requires no more than ten minutes and requires only three simple steps—cleanse, tone, and moisturize—each evening and morning.

Night Care

- **Cleanse**. Remove any makeup with cleansing cream or a natural makeup remover. Wash with mild soap or other cleanser, rinse, and pat dry.

- **Tone**. Apply a small amount of freshener(use an alcohol-free astringent if you have oily or blemished skin) to a cotton pad or ball. Begin at the décolleté (bust line) and gently apply over the neck area and face, using a patting motion.
- **Moisturise**. Splash on cool water or mist with a spray bottle. Blot, but do not dry completely—moisturiser magic relies more on retaining moisture than in providing it—then smooth on a few drops of your moisturiser.

Day Care

- Cleanse lightly to remove nighttime accumulations, refresh your face with a few splashes of water, and pat dry.
- Tone by applying a freshener or astringent. While your skin is still moist immediately after applying your freshener, alcohol free astringent, or water, apply a daytime moisturiser using gentle patting and smoothing motion.

• • •

10

How to Winterise Your Skin?

Winter is beauty's enemy. Overexposure to dry, cold wind also damages the skin. In addition to their dehydrating effects, cold and wind put pressure on the epidermis, the horny protective top layer of skin, which is composed of dead cells. When the cold and pressure are extreme, the dead cells desquamate–they burst–leaving the living, young cells of the dermis layer exposed prematurely to the elements. As a result, the unprotected cells become inflamed, causing a tingling sensation on the skin, a problem that is particularly common among the elderly in cold season.

Dry skin suffers more than oily skin, but every type of skin benefits from these defensive measures:

- Cold weather and cool winds aggravate dry skin condition; so adjust lifestyle and diet add warmth, lubrication, and moisture.
- Tone and moisture after each cleansing to preserve and replenish the moisture in your skin. Use a moisturising night nourisher every evening. Apply a daytime moisturiser around your eyes and on dry-skin areas each morning. Take fewer baths and showers in cold season to avoid dryness. When you do bathe, add few drops of essential oil to the water

to provide lubrication. Massage with oil before and after bathing.

- Add skin-pampering Ingredients to your bath to prevent skin dryness.
- Wait 30 minutes after bathing, or washing your face, before going out into frigid air. Splash your face with cool water when you come back inside. Extreme temperature changes can burst capillaries near the skin's surface.

• • •

11

How to Summarise Your Skin?

The sun has always been a prime offender against the skin, but in recent years its harmful effects have increased as the protective ozone layer has weakened. Solar radiation is a factor in cataracts, cell degeneration, and the breakdown of collagen and elastin, which leads to premature aging and wrinkles. It is the leading cause of skin cancer, and also increases free radical generation in the skin because it decreases production of antioxidant enzymes. When ingested and absorbed into the body they will cause hyper pigmentation if the skin is exposed to too much sun. Of course, summer heat aggravates, leading to increased skin sensitivity and sebaceous secretions.

In general, sensitive skin types tend to turn red rather than tan in the sun, and also develop freckles. Dry and oily skin types both tan easily. Nevertheless, nothing ages the skin more quickly than a sunburn, so individuals of every skin type should take precautions to protect themselves from the sun.

- Give your face an extra cleansing each day and always clean your face after strenuous activity. Warm weather means more active oil glands. Perspiration makes dirt cling to your skin.
- Use a "light" night cream and daytime moisturiser. Smooth on only a few drops to compensate for the

extra washing and perspiring that remove the skin's invisible shield. Use additional moisturiser when you travel by plane; pressurised air is excessively dry.

- Watch out for the sun; too much of it makes skin lined, leathery, and old before its time.
- Use a sunscreen with an SPF of 15 to 30, depending upon your skin. If you don't burn easily but do tan easily, use lower SPF. If you burn more easily than you tan, use higher SPF. Try not to use sunscreen unless you are in the sun, since it tends to increase skin sensitivity in general. Sesame and neem oil both are excellent natural sunscreens.
- Avoid sunbathing. If you do sunbathe, olive and coconut oils are natural tanning agents, since they absorb ultraviolet light and provide even colouring. A daily dose of B-complex vitamins also helps produce an even tan.
- After sunbathing, take a cool bath, adding a few drops rose, sandalwood, or vetiver essence to the water.
- To treat sunburned skin, rub on either crushed cucumber, cucumber juice, aloe vera juice, an ice infusion of elderflower and chamomile, or cold buttermilk.

12

Helpful Tips for Effective Skin Care

You can improve your looks at any age. Equipped with useful tips, a careful diet and regular exercise, you can make your face glow with health, beauty, and vitality; without having to ' resort to camouflage techniques. Face care varies with skin type. Here are some useful tips.

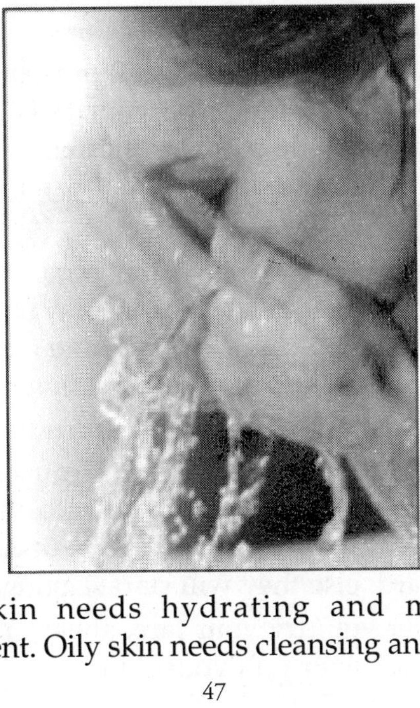

- Dry skin needs hydrating and moisturising treatment. Oily skin needs cleansing and freshening.

- Patchy skin needs smoothening and lightening treatment.
- Change in season requires a change in the skin care routine.
- To keep the skin glowing, drink at least 12-15 glass of ater per day.
- Your diet should be rich in raw vegetables and fresh fruits. These hydrate your skin.
- Protect yourself from the harshness of the sun. This is the main cause of skin discolouration, pigmentation and wrinkles.
- Exercise regularly: even a good walking routine will suffice. Exercise facial muscles regularly. Rotate your neck slowly, side to side, and loosen the facial muscles.
- Laugh loudly, it helps to exercise the facial muscles.
- Wash your face several times a day.
- Steam your face once a week to clean up clogged pores. After steaming, rub your face, forehead and neck vigorously to exfoliate the skin.
- Take Vitamin E for shadows and scars. But consult a doctor first.
- Once a fortnight go in for an elaborate cleansing and moisturising treatment by using any of the fruits and vegetables mentioned. The type and the nature of the treatment depends upon your skin type.
- "Feed" your skin. It requires nourishment too.
- Whenever you apply a lotion or cream or moisturiser, use gentle, swift, featherlike upward strokes. Do not use downward strokes or pull your facial muscles downward, else they will start sagging.
- Whenever you dry your face, always pat it dry. Do not rub, scrub or pull your skin.

- Avoid rapid or excessive weight loss.
- Ensure a good night's sleep. It rests and nourishes your skin.
- A diet rich in Vitamin A prevents a patchy, dry or rough skin. It is also good for people who have acne and pimples.
- Vitamin B prevents spots on the face.
- Strawberries are an instant cure for dry skin. Take a few strawberries, puree them. Add to this half cup milk and a tablespoon of glycerine. Shake well, pour in a jar and store in the refrigerator. Use this whenever the skin appears to be dry and taut. Apply on face, leave on for 10 minutes. Rinse. The skin is as soft like that of a baby.
- Your face is the most expressive, noticeable and also the most delicate part of the body. Normal facial expressions like frowning, raising of the eyebrows, wrinkling of the forehead, all this eventually lead to wrinkles. So make a facial massage as a regular routine to combat wrinkling.
- Use a moisturiser after exfoliation. It helps to reseal the skin and protects it from over drying.
- Prolonged use of alcohol based perfumes and deodorants can cause brown patches and dryness.
- Avoid going out in the direct sun when using a perfume. Spray onto clothes instead of directly on the skin.

• • •

13

Organic Skin Care

Many people would rather use completely natural way to care for their skin. This isn't really all that surmising, some of the less **natural skin care products** hurt your skin more than helps. They can cause irritation, dry skin, significantly reduces your skin's ability to produce the moisturising oils needed to correct what the chemicals do, and they can damage lipids.

For natural skin care, you obviously use completely natural things, like sea salt, lemons, and other completely natural things that do not damage your skin, but cleans it and helps it to heal.

First of all, there is sea salt. Sea salt works like Epsom salts to help clean skin and allow your skin to heal at a faster rate. Below is a sea salt recipe for your organic skin care that you can use on your body and feet. It will even help you achieve softer skin.

For the feet, you first mix a ¼ cup of sea salt to a bowl or pedicure dish filled with nice warm water. Let your feet soak as long as you feel they need, normally ten minutes will do, but if you are stressed a little longer will help you to relax. If you are looking for a real relaxing experience during this organic skin care endeavour then you can add between 10 and 15 drops of any essential oils that you choose. Some of the recommended oils are shown below, along with reasons why?

First and most recommended for feet is lavender. This organic skin care item helps to fight athletes foot and almost any other foot problems you may be having. It even works great as an antiseptic as well as a purifier. The amazing aromatic quality is both relaxing and stress reducing.

Next is lemon. Lemon helps the body to deep cleanse while renewing. This cleansing and refreshing aroma will help you to relax after a hard day on your feet.

Neroli is another good oil to use. This is an amazing treatment for people with dry and cracked skin and will help you to calm and restore your energy.

Finally there is tangerine. This amazing fruit has wonderful aromatic oils. It helps your nerves to calm while soothing your nervous system. This oil goes beyond natural skin care to aid in helping people suffering from depression to feel better overall.

In addition to the foot wash, you can turn this salt water relaxing method into a body wash by tripling the used ingredients. If you feel the need for a body scrub with it, you can take a handful of the sea salt you are using and rub it all over your body while you are soaking. You should try to avoid your eyes and face so that it doesn't sting. Rinse the scrub off before you are done.

If you are looking for a way to thoroughly clean your face you might try lemon. This won't cause damage to your skin but will clean any extra oil without drying up your skin.

• • •

14

Climatic Changes and Skin Care

Besides with increasing age, your skin can also change from day-to-day. The environment and the climatic conditions in which you live are major influences on the condition of your skin. Long-distance travel is a specially stressful situation for the skin. However, if you make simple adaptations to your skin care routine, you can stop problems before they start, avoiding the need for rescue operations that require time and effort.

Dry, Heated Atmospheres

Air-conditioning and central heating make life difficult for your skin. The humidity in some offices is lower than the Sahara Desert! As a result, the atmosphere robs your skin of precious moisture, leading to general dryness and flaking, and chapped-even cracked-lips.

Normal, Dry and Sensitive Skins

These skin types suffer especially in dry atmospheres. The skin on your face may feel tight and you will be able to see fine lines on its surface. If this happens, use a richer, more high-powered moisturiser.

Oily and Combination Skins

If your skin tends to be oily and your indoor environment stimulates the sebaceous glands and makes the situation worse, use an oil-free moisturiser, blot any oil coming to the surface of the skin with a tissue and be sure to cleanse thoroughly night and morning.

How to Overcome the Effects of a Dry, Hot Atmosphere?

- Place bowls of water near radiators. The drier the room, the faster the water will evaporate. Alternatively you could invest in a humidifier.
- Keep a check on the temperature indoors and, if possible, turn the thermostat down.
- Drink water throughout the day rather than tea or coffee.
- Remember that they are diuretics and cause water loss.
- Don't sleep in an over-heated room. This can cause fluid retention in the face, leaving you with a puffy complexion and bags under your eyes the next morning.

The Deep Freeze

Cold, harsh weather conditions are the worst environmental challenge your skin will face.

Chilly temperatures restrict the blood circulation to the skin, so it looks pale and devitalized. They also make the texture of your skin rough when touched and it often looks dull. The protective acid mantle is reduced too, as the glands are less active in cold weather. In addition, cold winds and dry atmospheres take moisture away from your skin. After the age of thirty your skin's moisture levels naturally decreases, so it is even more vulnerable to adverse environmental conditions.

The effects of cold weather has on your skin are as much as fourteen times worse when the air is also dry, and can be ten times worse in high winds.

If you are skiing, your face is in for an even tougher time. At high altitudes, the lack of oxygen increases the skin's sensitivity to cold and the sun's ultraviolet rays dehydrate and age the skin.

How to overcome the Effects of Cold Weather

- If you wash your face, do so at least half an hour before you go outdoors. This gives your skin a chance to dry thoroughly. If your face is slightly damp, the wind has an extra-drying effect.
- Wear a richer moisturiser.
- Apply night cream to replenish moisture lost from the skin during the day.
- If your skin is flaking, avoid abrasive scrubs. Use a very gentle complexion exfoliator.
- Remember to take care for your hands and nails, too, as the skin here can also suffer in cold weather.
- Always apply waxy lip salves or balms to your lips which are especially vulnerable to dehydration.
- Add oils and moisturising gels to your bath and apply body-lotions every day.
- Never come in from ice cold weather and immediately roast yourself in front of a hot fire, as you will dry your skin excessively; the rapid contrast in temperature can also break capillaries, leading to red thread veins.
- If you are skiing or are outside in sunny, but cold weather, apply protective lotions on any part of exposed skin. In cold weather you will not be warmed by the heat of the sun on your face so that it may be burning. If there is snow it will reflect on the sun, increasing its damaging effect. You will need special sun protection products if you are going out in sub-zero temperatures. Other products contain a higher

percentage of water and may freeze on the skin, breaking the tiny capillaries. Use products specifically formulated to protect the skin in cold and windy conditions and use sunblocks on your lips. Reapply sun protection products frequently during the day.

Humid Heat

In humid, hot climates, cleansing is a top priority in order to remove oil and dirt, especially if you have oily or problem-skin.

How to Overcome the Effects of Humid Heat

- Keep a mini skincare kit with you. Pack in it small or travel-sized bottles of wipe-off cleanser and toner and, if you need to, cleanse quickly at midday, morning and night, using tissues.
- Just use moisturiser where you need it and choose light or oil-free types rather than heavier creams.
- Wear a water-based foundation, especially if your skin is oily. If you prefer not to wear foundation during hot weather, just sweep on a little translucent or bronze powder to control and shine.
- Look out for oil-blotting lotions that can be worn under foundation to keep your skin matte and shine-free. Apply only over the T-zone.
- If you are working in a city, consider having facials more regularly to cleanse your skin of pollution residues. Your pores open up in hot weather and so absorb these residues more readily than when it is cooler.

Hot Dry Weather

Warm climates are not necessarily humid. When the weather is hot and dry, it is important to ensure that you protect your skin against moisture-loss by wearing a moisturiser.

Apply a light, oil-free moisturiser where your skin tends to dry out easily and reapply it during the day, if necessary.

Pollution

Air pollutants such as exhaust and industrial fumes, and indoor pollutants such as dust and cigarette smoke, are absorbed by the skin's hydrolipidic (water and oil) film.

Over time exposure to pollutants means that, instead of performing its role of protecting the skin, this film starts to act as a skin irritant which can result in weakened, compromised skin function and a complexion that becomes noticeably more sensitive.

Pollution also increases the production of free radicals which accelerate skin ageing. Cell inflammation also leads to damage. Some dermatologists believe that passive smoking is more damaging than the sun over long periods of time.

You should remember to cleanse your face thoroughly, but do so gently every evening. De-sensitizing facials, that also deep-clean the skin, are available in beauty salons.

Air purifiers are sold in department stores, chemist shops and health food stores. You can also surround yourself at home and in the office with plants which will absorb some of the pollutants.

Flying

The air in planes in notoriously dry, leaving you feeling dehydrated and lethargic and your skin drained of energy and moisture. The tissues beneath the skin can become congested, too, and puff up, making you feel even more uncomfortable.

How to Overcome the Effects of Flying

- As part of your final preparations before leaving, apply body lotion after you've showered or bathed. If you are travelling to a hot country, use self-tanning moisturiser will give your skin a colour boost for when you arrive.
- Carry a skin care kit in your hand luggage. As soon as you can, remove your make-up, freshen your skin with toner and spritz it with a mineral water spray. Apply moisturiser and eye gel to ease any tendency to puffiness. If you are on a long-haul flight, repeat this routine when your skin feels dry, or use a moisturiser with extended moisturising power-some moisturise the skin for up to twenty-four hours.
- Drink plenty of water and fruit juice to prevent dehydration.
- Avoid alcohol, tea, coffee and cola drinks as these actually have a diuretic effect.
- Move around as much as you can to stimulate your circulation.

In one test, carbon monoxide reduced cellular functioning by 24 percent, exhaust fumes reduced functioning by 65 percent and cigarette smoke affected it by 70 percent.

Moisturisers and make-up, that include 'anti-pollution complexes' with skin shielding, soothing and anti-inflammatory ingredients, are increasingly available.

These complexes include plant extracts such as horse chestnut, ginseng, linden flowers, seaweed and some vitamins, especially A, C, E and B5.

Check that your diet contains good quantities of vegetables and fruits that are high in the A, C and E vitamins too, to protect your skin-cells from the inside out.

Impairing the hydrolipic film can also leave the skin vulnerable to dehydration. Moisturisers, which restore suppleness and which provide a protective barrier (known as filmogenic) to cut down moisture loss, are particularly important in a polluted environment. These moisturisers should also contain ultraviolet filters.

• • •

15

Cleansing / Moisturising / Steaming

Procedures for caring your skin...........

Cleansing

If you want to keep your skin in good condition you should keep it on top priority.

A quick cleanse in the morning (to remove toxins that have reached the surface via the sweat glands) and a thorough cleanse at night are important for every skin type. Soap doesn't remove make-up and can be drying, so use soap-free cleansing bars, or wash-off or wipe-off cleansing creams instead. Toner, or freshener, removes the last traces of dirt and excess cleanser. Some toners contain alcohol to remove excess oil, but alcohol-free toners are a better choice. Toner containing alcohol can be drying and should be diluted even for oily skins.

Removing Eye Make-up

- Dab a little eye make-up remover on to two cotton wool pads. Never use tissue on eyes.
- Using one pad for each eye (to avoid the spread of infection), hold it against your lashes for a few seconds to dissolve the make-up.
- Supporting the skin by placing the fingers of your opposite hand on your brow, stroke in towards your

nose and down from your eyebrow. Don't move the pad up and out as you will pull the skin in the wrong direction.

Using Wipe-off Cleanser

- Warm the cleanser in your hands so that it doesn't go on cold.
- Smooth it over your face with your whole hand, starting at the neck and working up and out.
- Place your thumbs under your chin and work the cleanser in little circles with your index fingers around your nose and chin.
- Remove the cleanser by wiping it off gently with a soft tissue or a piece of cotton wool.

Using Wash-off Cleanser

- Dampen the skin with warm water and use the same movements given above to apply the cleanser.
- Rinse the cleanser off very thoroughly with comfortable warm running water. Water that is too hot will dehydrate the skin and causes broken capillaries.
- Pat your face dry with a tissue or a clean towel.

Using Toner

- Sweep the toner on to your face with a cotton wool pad, moving up and out, avoiding the eye area.
- Blot your skin dry with a tissue.

Moisturising

Moisturising are formulated to tackle different skin problems.

Creams help balance drier skin, while lotions and emulsions are designed for normal to oily complexions. Innovative, featherweight formulations are the latest trend-containing high-powered hydrating ingredients, they are suitable for evey skin type, except very dry.

Oil-free and gel moisturisers are perfect for oily complexions. Anti-ageing ingredients, such as ultraviolet filters, and nutrients, such as vitamins, are often added to moisturisers and serums to help protect the skin.

Night creams are useful from the age of twenty-five, especially for dry skins, but avoid very heavy creams as these can result in puffiness.

Moisturising the very delicate skin, surrounding the eyes, calls for special products. Your usual moisturiser may cause puffiness and stretch the skin. Eye gel is refreshing in the morning, and a little eye cream will strengthen the tissues at night. Pat on either, using the third and fourth fingers, tapping quickly but gently.

Your usual moisturiser is fine for your neck.

Quick Skin-care for Various Types of Skin

Select your type of skin from the following list and devote every day just five minutes to make your skin healthy and glowing.

Normal Skin

One hundred percent normal skin is a rare blessing.

- It is smooth textured with no visible pores.
- It shows no signs of dryness in youth.
- It has an even tone that is not too pale, sallow or red.
- It will tend towards dryness with age and as a result of external influences.

Morning

- Cleanse using a wipe-off or wash-off cleanser for normal-to-dry skin.

- Tone using alcohol-free toner one a water-moistened cotton ball.
- Hydrate with a moisturiser for normal skin.

Evening

- Remove your eye make-up first, then cleanse, as above, but more thoroughly.
- Apply moisturiser or a lightweight night lotion.

Dry Skin

- It has a fine, matter texture.
- It may be on the sensitive side.
- There are usually no open pores.
- It is more prone to fine lines and wrinkles than other skin types.
- It is more vulnerable to the effects of central heating and sunlight.
- Very fair skin is often dry

5-minute Skin-care

Morning

- Cleanse quickly, using a wipe-off cleanser for dry skin.
- Tone, using alcohol-free toner on water-moistened cotton ball.
- Hydrate with a moisturiser for dry skin, preferably one containing a broad-spectrum sunscreen. Avoid and protect your eyes.

Evening

- Remove your eye make-up.
- Cleanse as above.
- Apply a night-cream.

Oily Skin

- It has open pores.
- It will shine an hour or so after washing.
- It may look oily on waking.
- It has a tendency to spots and blackheads.
- It is less susceptible to wrinkles than other skin types.

5-minute Skin-care

Morning

- Cleanse quickly, using a wipe-off cleanser for normal-to-oily skin or a soap-free cleansing bar. Rinse very thoroughly.
- Tone, using a toner that should be diluted if it contains alcohol so that it is not too drying. Moisten your cotton wool with water.
- Moisturise where needed, using an oil-free or gel moisturiser.

Evening

- Remove your eye make-up, then cleanse as above, but more thoroughly.
- Apply moisturiser just where needed.

Sensitive Skin

- Looks fragile and translucent.
- It is generally dry.
- It may have freckles.
- It tends to become flushed, blotchy and irritated in extremes of temperature or through using harsh cleansing products.
- It may suffer from broken red veins, dermatitis, allergies.

5-minute Skin-care

Follow the programme for dry skin.

Special Tips

- Look for hypoallergenic products that are scentfree.
- Before trying a new product do a patch test. Rub a good amount on to your shoulder and leave it one overnight. If there is no sign or irritation, apply some to your neck and wait again. If there is no reaction, then the product will probably be safe to use on your face.

Black Skin

- Tends towards extremes of oiliness or dryness which can be a real problem, since these conditions are more visible against a darker complexion. Dry black skin may appear greyish in colour.
- It needs very gentle care as face scrubs, spots, ear piercing and hair removal can make the supply of melanin uneven, leading to skin that is darker or lighter in some places than others.

5-Minute Skin-care

Follow the programme for dry or oily skins.

Special Tips

- If your skin is sensitive, use toners that do not contain alcohol, and choose fragrance-free products.
- If flaky, grey-looking skin is a problem, gently use a flannel to slough the skin, or use a peel-off mask.

Olive Skin

- It tends towards oiliness and often has larger pores.
- Any sallowness is due to lack of pink pigment.

5-Minute Skin-care

Follow the programme for oily skins.

A Mixture of Skin Types

Skin may develop the characteristic of several skin types as a result of incorrect treatment and environmental skin hazards. For example:

- An oily, spotty skin can also suffer from the dry skin problems of fine surface lines and flaking, it you work in an over-heated office, perhaps smoke or eat a poor diet, or use harsh and abrasive cleaners (over-enthusiastic scrubbing with anti-bacterial products can aggravate oily skin and dry the surface).

Fast Skin Stimulants

Get your skin glowing with fast and easy treatments you can do at home.

Exfoliation

Exfoliators, or skin sloughers, are speedy skin improvers. By removing the dead cells from the surface of the skin, face 'scrubs' make your skin smoother and brighter in seconds. They also help skin that is prone to spots, stay clearer and increase the cell turnover so the skin looks younger for longer.

It is important to choose a product that is very gentle so that the dermis do not scratch the skin.

Tips for using an Exfoliator

- Use a facial scrub on cleansed, damp skin.
- Rest your thumb against your skin (this ensures that you don't use the full power of your arm) and use very light, circular movements.
- Never rub your skin until it changes colour and do not use exfoliators near your eyes.

- If your skin is fair, sensitive or very fine, use a gentler peel-off mask, instead of a facial scrub to lift away dead cells and revitalize your complexion.
- Exfoliation is very useful for black skin, which can look ashen in colour, but a peel-off mask is better than a face scrub, as black skin is vulnerable to changes in pigmentation and face scrubs can trigger this, if too abrasive.
- Although facial scrubs help prevent your skin breaking out in spots, do not use them if your skin is already inflamed or infected, as you may spread the infection. This is true for the body too.

Marvellous Masks

Masks are a really good way to glaze up skin, in no time at all.

Cleansing masks, which often contain clay or fruit, absorb excess oils. The enzymes in fruits such as papaya have a deep-cleansing action and leave the skin glowing.

Moisturising masks give drier skin a real boost, smoothing out fine lines and refreshing the face. Some moisturising masks also contain toning and firming ingredients, such as seaweed, herbs and aromatherapy oils and are excellent as complexion-improves before a party or after a late night.

Steaming

Steaming is an effective way of cleansing the skin. You can add herbs, such as soothing camomile.

If you have sensitive skin or skin that is prone to broken capillaries. However, specialists recommend that you do not cleanse with steam.

Tips for Steaming

- Cleanse your skin first.
- Pour water that is almost boiling into a bowl and lean over the steam. Draping a towel over your head and the bowl will prevent steam escaping.
- Be very careful not to get too close to the water (stay 30 cm, 12 or so away). Do not steam for more than a few minutes.
- Apply a cleansing mask afterwards, while your skin is still warm, or cleanse your skin again and massage moisturiser into it.

• • •

16

Keep your Health and Beauty without Much Expenses

In past years, the **women** simply "tweak" their faces with a little mascara and lipstick. This is because, at that era food was more natural. Eating is done only on rare occassions. The families ate home-cooked meals. Vegetables and fruits were picked from the garden. The meat is not pumped full of hormone. Life is less stressful. All this promotes the health and welfare. Do you remember when obesity is a rarity? Most women generally feel good about their looks and figures. All that has changed today. Covering up acne, rosacea, large pores, oily skin, is the norm. We have entered into a principle, "would not be seen by anyone and did not keep my makeup" era. Most women generally feel good about their looks and figures. Most **personal care products** containing sodium laureth sulfate or sodium lauryl ether sulfate.Very few problems of skin care are not really fixable.

Much of the mass produced **food** we eat today may be of lower quality than that of yesteryear, it will satisfy your hunger, but may not give the food they need to feel and look good. The nutrients in the food could have been reduced or eliminated, sometimes even by rigorous methods of production and processing. Eat the way nature intended, processed foods should be avoided whenever possible and avoid junk food, stick to vegetables, fruits (fruits and vegetables can also be beneficial), grains, seeds and vegetables, oily fish and some meat and cheese. Mediterranean diet are said to be the healthiest, so do not forget the olive oil! Well yes, olive oil is a fat but fat is a healthy one of the essential omega fatty acids.

The next debate is in organic foods, these are more expensive but it is never the least free of pesticides, antibiotics and growth hormones, which can sometimes be detrimental to health. Organic food is often taste much better too. Try shopping around, farm shops can be worthwhile to try and of course on how to treat a growth of their own power not only be healthier, but also self-satisfying. If you eat a lot of organic beef and want to try you might like to cut meat and not be used as a central element of many foods.

The most important thing you can do when applying **makeup** is to start with a clean face. A clean face gives you the perfect canvas to apply the rest of their **cosmetics**. A dirty face will make it much more difficult to apply makeup and cosmetics. Clean faces also help keep your skin clear and healthy-looking when it comes to health and beauty. After carefully cleaning the face (please take some time and make sure it is properly cleaned), are applied to the base smoothly and evenly. Foundation when applied correctly, it must not appear to be running it – this is a good way to start measuring to see if they have done correctly or not. The aim of the foundation is to smooth your skin colour to cover any blemishes and to help you put your cosmetics on simpler and more effective. Your face should feel light and natural and not caked with foundation in. If it is clear that you are using foundation or your face will feel as if you were plastered, and then, believe me, you have too! It's also good to consider if you are using the kind of makeup to the skin. For foundation to work properly, you must match your skin tone as closely as possible. If you have trouble choosing the background colour, and then talk to a cosmetics consultant at a local department store or stores. If you only had a little too much then the basis on which may stain the skin with a tissue to remove excess, without having to start again, this will save you much time.

Beauty bar soaps and cleaners have become the method of choice for most women. But just because something is popular is not the best option. Looking at the residue left over in the sink after washing your face, you recognize what I'm talking about. This residue is responsible for most of the problems of skin care.

• • •

17

How Refrigerator Can Help to Refresh your Skin?

You've seen the advertisements of women lounging with wrapped up hair, cream covered skin, and cucumbers over their eyes. This wasn't just to enhance relaxation by blocking the light. Cucumbers, along with other items commonly found in your **refrigerator,** are a home made alternative to some of the skin and beauty products you're used to.

Cucumbers sliced and placed over your eyes have long been used as treatment to decrease puffiness. Their high water and sodium content help to cool your skin while pulling the excess water from around your eyes, resulting in a smoother and less puffy appearance. Make sure you thoroughly wash the **cucumber** before putting it anywhere near your face.

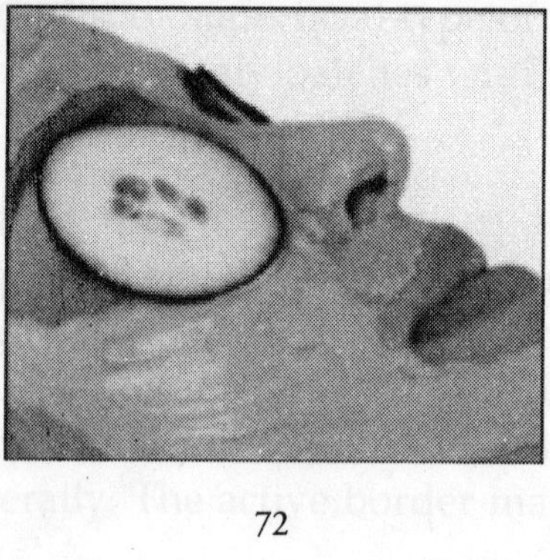

Something else you're probably familiar with for non-beauty reasons is caffeine. Also at home puffy-eye remedy, **tea bags** are used in place of **cucumbers**. Other skin products are now listing caffeine as an ingredient to be applied beyond just your face. While it can decrease the redness of your skin, many are using it in creams and lotions that target decreasing cellulite.

As your skin is soaking up **cucumbers** or tea, the dryness of your hair might start to seem painfully obvious. Deep **conditioners** can get very expensive, and often leave you with the same brittle hair you had to begin with. Mayonnaise is much cheaper, and is widely recognized as one of the best ways to liven up your hair and give it an optimal sheen. The common consensus is to go for the heavy stuff—skip the "lite" versions when it comes to your hair. Leave it in for up to a half hour, but find the duration that is best for you. If the smell is absolutely unappealing, a small amount of vanilla extract is recommended to dull it a bit.

As unconventional as using food for **beauty** may seem, many swear by using their own home made products, and these have stood the test of time for a reason.

• • •

18

Tips to Improve your Skin through Proper Nutrition

If you want to **improve your skin, proper nutrition** is one of the best ways to do this instead of spending lots of money on products that may not work. To improve your skin, you can include the following:

Red Wine

Red wine has collagens that help prevent wrinkles from forming on your skin. It also relaxes the skin and promotes blood flow which is essential to get a healthy glow. Take about one glass while you have dinner but remember to practice moderation because the more red wine you take does not necessarily mean you will have better results.

Green Tea

Green tea has the same effect as red wine on the skin's collagen. It strengthens the skin collagen to prevent wrinkles and it is advisable to take about 2 or 4 cups to enjoy the benefits of green tea on your skin.

Omega 3 Fatty Acids

These fatty acids will keep the cell membranes in your skin healthy and also give you protection from any damage from UV rays from the sun. The best sources that you can get them from include trout, salmon and sardines. If you do not like fish you can get the omega 3 fatty acids from flaxseeds, walnuts or eggs that have been fortified with omega 3.

Vitamin E

Vitamin E will also protect the skin's cell membrane and guard you from the damaging UV rays just like the omega 3 fatty acids. Guacamole and avocados are a great source of vitamin E. Other sources that will give you the vitamin E to improve your skin include nuts, seeds, wheat germ and fortified cereals.

Vitamin A

This vitamin will repair and help your skin grlow while also protecting it from sun damage. Foods that contain this vitamin include sweet potatoes, mangos, carrots, apricots and pumpkins.

Vitamin C

This nutrient helps to produce collagen in the skin to make your skin firmer. Some of the sources include oranges, strawberries, broccoli, lemons and sweet peppers.

Whole Grains

Eating whole grains will help to prevent wrinkles by reducing any elevation of blood sugar which leads to the growth of wrinkles.

Selenium

Selenium delays the skin aging process and also gives protection from the damaging effects of the sun. This nutrient also improves the elasticity and quality of your skin. To get selenium you can eat tuna, wheat germ, crab or Brazil nuts.

It is also advisable to drink more than eight glasses of water each day to help remove toxins from your body. The toxins often make your skin look dull and unhealthy.

When cooking, use cold pressed oils to get the maximum benefit for your **skin**. Sugar, fast foods and snacks that have no nutritional value should be avoided if you want to improve your skin. If you have any reaction on your skin because of a certain food, you should eliminate it to improve your skin. Garlic, asparagus and onions contain sulfur that is helpful to the skin and should be included in meals.

● ● ●

19

How to Apply Face Masks?

One of the ways you can ensure that your skin remains healthy, supple and smooth is by using a **face mask** on a regular basis. This can be done once a week or twice a week to **remove any excess oil, reduce the size of the skin pores**, improve moisture content and nourish your skin.

If you have any whiteheads or blackheads, the face mask will help to reduce them. The **facial mask** can be home-made or manufactured. To get the benefits of a facial mask, make sure that you use it in the right way. Choose a time when there are no interruptions around you.

Follow the following tips when you are applying your facial mask

- If you are using a new brand of facial mask, try it on a less visible part of your skin such as behind the ear; especially if your skin is sensitive.
- Hair should be tied away from the face with a headband to prevent the facial mask from getting on your hair. It will also ensure that you apply the mask on each part of the face.
- To make the mask more effective, clean your face and neck meticulously using a gentle cleanser for about

two minutes and rinse using water that is lukewarm. Let your skin dry off completely to make sure that the mask is applied on skin that is clean and dry.

- Steam your face for about two or five minutes to open your pores to ensure the mask works effectively.
- The best way to apply the facial mask is by using your fingers since the warmth on your fingers makes it easy to spread it. Put some of the face mask on your palm and spread it on your face.
- Begin applying the mask on your forehead while lightly rubbing it on the skin. Work the mask down your face including the cheeks, chin and nose until you get to the neck. The mask should never be put on the lips or skin on the eyes.
- Once you have done this, you can leave the mask on for some time as instructed on the pack you bought it in. If you had made the facial mask yourself, you should make sure that you leave it until it sets properly. Avoid making facial expressions while you still have the mask on. It is preferable if you lie on your bed and keep your eyes closed.

- When the mask has set and the required time is over, you should rinse out the facial mask using some warm water. After rinsing, you can use a cleanser that is mild on your face to make sure that you remove the facial mask completely.
- When you remove the entire facial mask, you should use a soft towel to pat your face and then apply some moisturiser on it. A tonic or a hydrating cream can also be used on the skin once you remove the mask.

• • •

20

Peeling to Improve your Skin

Is the most revolutionary concept in facial and body aestheticism imperfections **Chemical peelings** are made with topical formulas which are used exclusively by doctors in their clinics, and are different from each other in their composition accordingly to the results expected.

They are prescribed for the treatment of several skin pathologies, such as:

- Wrinkles
- Dyschroa
- Dehydration
- Aging and Photo aging (solar damage)
- Very greasy skin

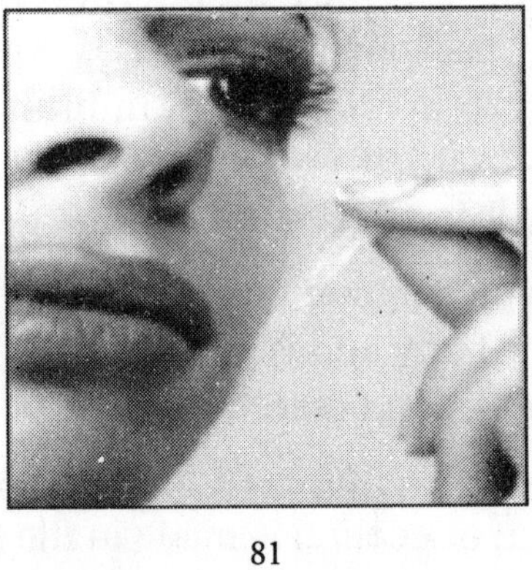

- Acne.
- Vanish scars
- Diminish strias
- Gives light and softens skin

The objective is to make a change, improving skin appearance from the inside, which means that the product used works inside the skin stimulating what is needed to return to the skin's natural balance and increase collagen and elastin production; and the essential components to keep the skin healthy. This effect appears as a remarkable change in a short time and depends on the kind of peeling used and the depth of it.

Applying this kind of products stimulates the regeneration of the skin from the depth layers of it is and accelerates the superficial damaged parts.

There are uncountable formulations from the simple ones, old and still valid alpha hydroxyl acids till the modern ones, such as the lacto bionic acid, which one to choose depends on the symptoms and which skin layer is going to be treated to achieve the most convenient effect.

Within the concept of peeling is included the dermabrasion treatment, which uses a rotatory abrasive device of micro crystals of aluminium oxide or with diamond tips which is widely used to improve and eliminate strias.

This kind of treatment is useful not only for the face but also for the body and is usually combined with others to achieve the desired objectives.

The treatment requires of a previous preparation of the skin, which in general is made in the first session and subsequent home care with products especially indicated for each case in particular.

Skin recovery depends on the kind of peeling done, that means the dermic layer to which it was directed to, and the frequency it is done will be according to the objective so as the agent used during the procedure.

• • •

21

Thermage Face Lift

If you are a person whose skin is just beginning to age, and looks like it may need a facelift soon, you may find that a **thermage face lift** is something you want to look into as an alternative.

A thermage facelift is not actually a facelift; it is what you should do to avoid a facelift or the surgery that comes with the facelift. For most people who are just beginning to really show their age, this will work. However, if you are in desperate need of a facelift and far advanced into aging, it will not work as well. That means, if you are looking for drastic results you should look into an actual facelift, but if you are merely looking for a little bit of an improvement, and not the perfect pace, then the thermage face lift will work for you nicely.

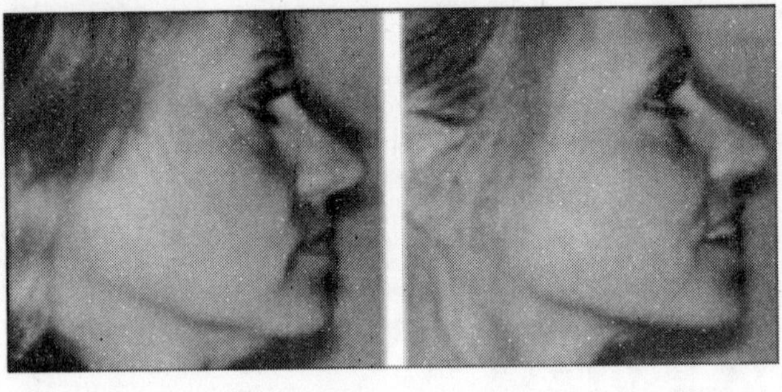

The thermage face lifts are really heating, and cooling to avoid burning your skin, applied strategically to your skin in order to help tighten your skin and which reduces wrinkles, the turkey like neck, or some of your loose skin. It may even reduce any acne or acne scars you may have, as well as improving your jowling and tightening your jaw line.

When you undergo a **thermage face lift**, your doctor will begin by using local anesthesia in strategic places all over your face. Depending on how much anesthesia and how high the treatment setting is you may feel little to know pain or discomfort during the treatment. Then a grid will be applied to your face in order to guide the treatment. And then starts the treatment. Your doctor will hold a treatment tip over your skin. This tip will deliver radio frequencies and the cooling that is needed to keep your skin from burning.

For the most part, if you are looking for better results then you will need higher settings on the thermage machine. In some cases though, it may just be that you are recommended that you use a mild setting and the just undergo yet another treatment in six months. The first treatment will improve your skin for that long, if not.

• • •

22

Non Surgical Face Lift

There are two main types of **non-surgical face lifts** that have been looked at and proven effective for years. Though there are others that are now being tried, the two that are proven are the ones we will talk about.

The two main types of non-surgical face lifts are thermage face lifts and titan face lifts. Both of these work alike in the sense that they both require the heating, and of course cooling to avoid burns, of the skin, however they each heat the skin with a different method. For both of these results will continue for at least six months after the treatments, and then you can get another one, or you are done, depending on what your doctor says.

The thermage face lift uses radiofrequency energy to strategically heat and cool the skin to allow your skin to become healthier looking for at least six months. This treatment usually only takes once for good, if not great, results, and then you don't have to do it again for years to come. However, there are times when a doctor decides that it is a good idea to go in for a second treatment after a six month period, though for most people this doesn't happen.

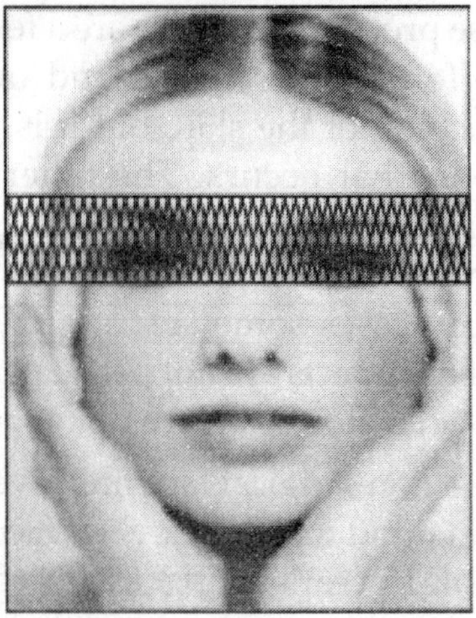

The Titan face lifts works by using infrared to heat and cool the skin on your face (Skin Tightening). For this, it could take between two and three treatments to get the full effect of the face lift capabilities that you are looking for, but there are people who still feel that infrared is superior to other systems. This is because they believe that you are less likely to suffer from any of the after effects that are possible with the non-surgical face lifts.

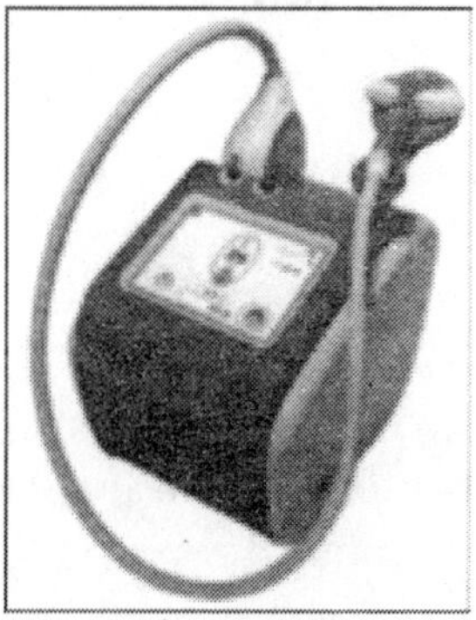

For the most part, pain is not a real issue with using either system, though it is possible for some people who are sensitive. There is also little to no downtime for people after one of these procedures. There are a few cases where the patient suffers from redness and or swelling or temporary blanching of the skin, but it is very rare that anything beyond that occurs. The other possibilities, though they are rare, are a permanent change in the pigment, bumps or blistering, or even skin depressions. In extremely rare cases some scarring is also possible. Though most of the effects are not permanent, it is always better to talk to your doctor before doing anything.

Though these non-surgical face lifts give good results, one must keep in mind that they are not face lifts. You can not expect to look 15 years younger than you did the day before. What you can expect though is that your skin will have less acne, the scars will be less pronounced, and your skin will become a little tighter and lifted compared to what it is. These changes will come over a time period of about 6 months, though some cases show that your skin continues to improve even after that.

• • •

23

Natural Home Made Cosmetic Tips

Beauty is one of the most discussed topics as it affects how people carry on their day-to-day lives. In almost all societies beauty is a universal thing that everyone unanimously agrees that it's a treasured possession. With that in mind, lots of money is spent on purchasing **beauty products** some of which end up making the user worse due to the chemicals contained in them.

Since time immemorial people have invented **homemade remedies** to use in various beauty treatments. This has especially been encouraged by the fact that people are becoming aware that most of the **beauty treatments** available on the shelves contain harmful chemicals that cause very adverse health effects especially if used for long periods.

Some Tips on How to Make Natural Home-made Cosmetics:

For a soft skin, **tea tree oils, aloe vera** and **neem plants** extracts can be used to make a natural skin moisturiser. They are especially useful to people with dry skin conditions as their special nutrients will promote good health of the skin and make it smoother and younger.

For naturally dark hair, chemicals such as henna are recommended as it also acts as a hair conditioner that gives the hair both body and strength. Another plant called Salvia Oficinalis can be used to make the hair darker. The treatment is made by mixing 15 grams of the plant in a litre of water. It's then kept for two hours and later strained before being poured on the hair. This mixture should stay for half an hour and then the hair is rinsed with a generous amount of water.

For a **skin moisturiser**, beeswax or honey is applied in the skin and then left for a period of 30 minutes. For best results, the **honey** should be unprocessed or if processed, should not contain any chemicals.

A mixture of ripe avocádos and the white part of the egg can be used to make a hair conditioner. The mixture is kept for a period of two hours so that the two ingredients can blend in. Its then applied on the already cleaned hair and can stay for one hour or more depending on the wish of the user.

For brighter and cleaner eyes, a cucumber is sliced in small bits then placed on the eyes. These slices are believed to suck out impurities from the eyes. The **eucalyptus** and

mint plants are used for fresher breath. This remedy is quite simple and needs no mixtures. The person should simply chew either the leaves or small twigs of these plants for instantaneous results. This remedy was actually used long before toothpaste was invented.

For relaxing fragrant bath, ingredients such as **lavender** and **Salvia Officinal** are put in a muslin bag and hanged from a hot water tap such that the water passes through it. This extracts the **natural oils** and the fragrance of the herbs into the water. The extracts can also be used when doing a relaxing body massage and also for relieving rheumatism.

• • •

24

Easy Beauty Solutions

Summer Care: Wash your face with water after every 2 hours to avoid the grease on your skin. You can wash your face with just plain water, and then rub ice on your face.

Hair Loss: Boil 250 ml of mustard oil in a thin vessel. Add 60 gms of heena leaves gradually and continue boiling till they are burnt in the oil. Filter and store this mixture in the bottle. Massage hair regularly with this oil to prevent hair loss.

Anti-wrinkle: A mixture of juice of a quarter cucumber, egg white of 1 egg, a teaspoon lemon juice and a teaspoon of vodka makes an excellent anti-wrinkle lotion. Apply on your face and wash off after 10 minutes. Use at least twice a week.

Pimple-pimple: To get rid of your pimple scars from the face apply tomato pulp every day and wash off after an hour.

For Glowing Skin: Mix equal quantity of almond, rose water, glycerine and lemon juice. Apply on face and keep overnight. Wash off in the morning, first with warm water and then with cold water, to give a glowing effect to your face.

Skin Tonic: Mix together 1 egg yolk, 1 tsp honey and a pinch of turmeric and apply it for half an hour. You can preserve this mixture in fridge for around 20 days.

• • •

25

Seasonal Makeup

All seasons have their unique style, technique and type of makeup that may look out of place in other climatic and weather conditions. Winter makeup may look and prove very laughable and difficult to manage during the monsoons while makeup for summers may leave a person looking quite pale and colourless in a Christmas party! This section has come up with some very handy tips to apply appropriate makeup and look pretty in all seasons. Simple skin care can also keep you free of many worries such as dry and cracked lips. Use a bit of petroleum jelly and a soft bristle toothbrush to exfoliate any dead skin from the lips. Apply Vitamin E oil over them to make them look soft and kissable. Vitamin E oil is good for your nails, hair and skin in general too.

Acne is a common problem in summer, especially for people with oily skin. However, they can be easily treated too. Mix one spoon of sea salt in 4 ounces of warm water and use the solution to clean the area and cover it for 2 to 3 minutes using a cotton ball twice or thrice. Then pat the area dry. Sexy beach girls on screen always have beautiful lustrous hair that you think is impossible with all that sun, sand, wind and salt. Well, here is the trick. Braid your hair in as many parts as you want depending how many waves and curls you want. Then, go for a swim in the ocean and let them dry in the breeze naturally. Open up the braids and run your fingers through hair for the beautiful look. Champagne rinse plays up blonde highlights while beer conditioning adds shine to hair. So, now you know all those bottles are not only for drinking and having fun.

Thin slices of lemon in a tub of warm water remove dead skin, help in cleansing, hydrates skin and give you a wonderful citrus aroma. Baking soda absorbs excess moisture and works as an excellent deodorant. Body moisturisers with shimmer and tanning lotions are great for showing off your beautiful legs on beach. Summer and hot weather means more skin on the show and greater use of body makeup such as tanning powder and lotions that make arms, legs and shoulders look more athletic and sexy. These are also great for covering up any freckles or skin imperfection when going for bolder fashions. Winter is the best loved season by all women for there is no more need to worry about sweat smudging our carefully applied makeup and also allows us to go for a lot more brighter colours and fashions we have always wanted to play with. The colour range is largest for cold chilly winters ranging from neutrals such as white, light grays to charcoal gray, black, taupe, navy, true blue, royal blue, turquoise, royal purple, true green, emerald green, pine green, hot pink, magenta, fuchsia, burgundy, blue-red, true-red and icy colours such as icy green, icy yellow, icy aqua, icy violet, icy pink and icy blue. Silver jewelry looks best in winters.

Monsoon Makeup

In monsoons, dense makeup has a risk of being smudged and washed out severely and so light and sheer makeup is more advisable. Use waterproof mascara, transfer-resistant lipsticks and waterproof liners and may even use waterproof foundation, if it is a must for you.

Summer Makeup

Summer is the time to give your body the healthy tan and protect it from the horrors of sunburn, baked and dry lips and even sun-scorched skin cancer! There are some makeup disasters that can happen in summer sun and a relaxing beach noon that we do not pay adequate attention too.

Winter Makeup

There are so many people who dread winter for the mere reason that it brings a challenge to maintaining healthy and well-moisturiser skin. Extra care and attention is needed during the winter season, because during the cold months, the oil glands situated just below the surface of the skin tend to become relatively inactive and produce less moisture than usual.

• • •

26

Beauty for the Over-aged

Looking beautiful is every woman's everyday dream. They say beauty is in the eyes of the beholder. This is not the best way to perceive beauty, beauty is something that we nurture and need to look after daily. Women advancing in age are very worried when it comes to choosing the best products for their skin. As a woman gets older her skin becomes sensitive and will tend to react to various beauty products in the market.

What range is a woman regarded as over age. An **over age woman s** age will range from 50 years old going downwards. The first thing an over aged woman needs to have in order to attain beauty is to possess an **anti-aging products**. Another key thing is to make sure that you have got the right product that will auger well with your skin type. Old aged women can either have one of these three types of skin type's oily skin, dry skin or normal skin. Knowing your skin type is one thing you need to do so that you can know which anti-aging cream or powder you need to go for. Women over age are nowadays turning to anti-aging products such as chemical peels and **antioxidants**.

Beauty tips for women over aged will help them find out deeper secrets of how they can shed ten years from

their faces. The second thing a woman over age should know is that the eyes are the most key noticeable elements in the face and thus they should be taken care of. You do not want to go out with heavy and droopy eyed. The best way to take care of the eyes is to have enough rest and wash them properly. There are older age women with different types of eyes take for example, some have squinty eyes, others have far apart eyes and some have too close together eyes. The best way to take care of such problems is to wear the right eye make up, you will be surprised at how much eye make up will conceal. There are older age women who have dark circles around their eyes and they occur as a result of ageing. The best tip for this is to buy an **anti-wrinkle eye cream** which will ensure that the complexion on the eyes is even with that of the face.

Many older age women do not wash or cleanse their skin every day. Beauty tips for women over aged should be kept in mind, wash and cleanse your skin everyday, and never sleep with any make up on. The best way to clean your face is to first find the best moisturiser which removes the entire make up from the face and unblocks pores. Luke warm water is the best to clean your face. Be extra cautious when buying beauty soaps, some are counterfeit and do not meet the standards they claim. Manicure your nails and choose nice dress codes and with these tips you are destined to portray beauty all the way.

The way you wear your hair will also enhance your beauty. Hair colour and also hair style will tell much about you. Choose colours and make-up that will make you look cool. Do not over do make-up by applying too much dark colour.

• • •

27

Seven Beauty Tips for Teens

Although young people often seem to be bothered by advice from their folks, some useful advice is worth taking especially when it comes to **beauty tips for teens**. Magazines contain a lot of information most of which has been tested by our folks hence they know what is good for us and what is not. Here are some of the beauty tips for teens that older people always try to suggest to the younger generation.

1. Do not skip the foundation. Skipping the foundation will be bad for your body apart from making it appear natural. Use a concealer to top the blemished and then have and use it lightly. Avoid rubbing it. Put a

pad on your middle finger and try pat it into your **skin**. If you have **acne**, this is what you need to do.

2. Never apply make-up on your lips and eyes at the same time. If you have applied make-up heavily on your eyes, put a light gloss on your lips. Some people like the drama that comes with dry lipstick. Line your eyes lightly and then maintain a balance in terms of the amount of **make-up** you use. You don't want to look like a crown.
3. **Less make-up is better.** Applying too much make-up is not good at all. It is one of the crucial beauty tips for teens to adopt. In fact, if you make it a habit of applying many different types of make-ups on a daily basis, you are going too far with your quest for better looks. Instead of using Mascara and liners on a daily basis, you ought to tone the whole package down and settle for occasional mascara for tackling blemishes and gloss which could be complemented by some blush pops during winter.
4. Let your **hair** remain natural. If you have very dark hair, try and make your look a bit lighter through the use of highlights which are rather on the lighter side. Do not lighten the hair. Let it remain **natural**. Having maintained some natural air into your hair is something to be proud of.
5. Vaseline is cheap and best for you if **removing eye make-up** seems to be a problem. If you need to massage your lips, use a toothbrush. A tooth brush is a very efficient tool for making the lips supple and soft. A toothbrush makes your tooth very smooth such that applying make up becomes an enjoyable task.
6. Have long **layers** no matter the type of your hair. You can choose either wavy or straight. Sometimes super

curly is a good option for you. These are the layers that make very thin layer appear very thick and attractive. The hair does not look as if you dyed it using some crude chemicals.

7. If you have acne, visit a dermatologist. This is the professional has all the beauty tips for teens from a professional level. This is a medical problem that requires a medical solution rather than an aesthetic one.

• • •

28

Celebrities Makeup Secrets

Light…camera…action! Thousands of people are watching at your face on TV, your body, your outfit and your hair. It's not that simple to be a **celebrity**. Artist know that it is a part of the game to be constantly exposed to everybody's looks 24 Hours. For this reason, they spend an amazing amount of time in improving their looks. Now we know, thought, that bottox is not everything in Hollywood…let's dig into some of its most well kept **beauty secrets**:

- Supermodel Cindy Crawford moisturizes her skin constantly; she takes her atomiser everywhere. It contains the exact same amount quantities of mineral water and milk.
- Jennifer Love Hewitt fights acne with tooth-paste. She applies it on her spots before going to bed and says they are gone the next morning.
- Demi Moore goes beyond that, being 16 years older than her husband Ashton Kutcher, she resorts to…leeches! Ex Bruce Willis' wife says that after getting used to the bites, she could feel how her blood became toxins free.
- Another actress, Catherine Zeta Jones keeps her teeth pure white by brushing them with crushed

strawberries; and she moistures her hair with olive oil. Does she spend a lot of time in the kitchen?

- Nicole Kidman gives her hair blueberry baths to keep it smooth and glossy and Julia Roberts dips her nails in olive oil to keep them healthy and strong.
- Penelope Cruz sleeps eight hours a day and avoids caffeine, and Shakira mixes honey, sugar and lemon to scrub her body.
- Jennifer Aniston uses sugar and water to smooth her lips and combs her hair with wild boar combs.
- And the one that can't help but mentioning is the one that has the recipe for eternal youth… Madonna. Always at the forefront, not only music-wise, but because she was one of the first ones to use Pilates. Hers is a microbiotic diet, she does not eat meat, wheat or sugar. She never sunbathes and treats her skin with diamond edges twice a month. But that is not all…her ex-husband, Guy Ritchie, revealed that before going to bed, Madonna covers her body with moisturising creams and then gets dressed in a thermo suit that potentiates the moisturising effects.
- Victoria Beckham does something similar. She applies cream to her hand and feet and wears gloves and socks in bed.

It is neither simple nor natural, isn't it? Investing in these little secrets take a great deal of time, money and perseverance; however, and even when it sound like a cliché, when it's time to go out, it is our attitude that counts the most…and having people that love us just the way we are.

Without make up, no photoshop…they are girls just like everyone else!

• • •

29

Spa Like Treatment

Cleansing is a very important step in skin care and unlike soaps; cleansers will help you get rid of makeup and impurities from your face without removing your skin's natural oils. Cleansers are usually applied on the skin and rinsed or wiped off to leave the skin moisturised.

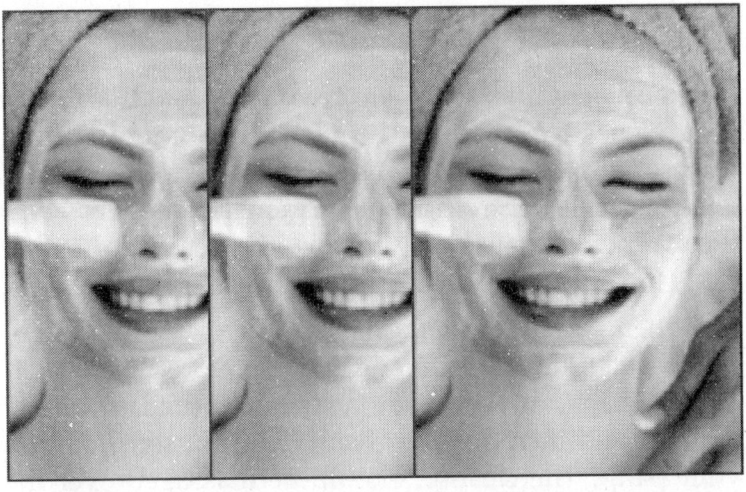

There are various cleansers available in the market in form of foams, lotions and creams to suit all types of skin. If you are looking for a cleanser that will pamper your skin to leave you feeling like you just went to the spa, you should try a warming cleanser. Warming cleansers are self-heating and are made using unique formulas that combine the potential of facial washes and the relaxing feeling you get after a **spa treatment**.

The formulations use micro-beads which are then activated to warm your skin. When the skin is warmed, the pores open up allowing the cleanser to clean deeper. Apart from cleansing, warming cleansers also have other benefits that include exfoliating and moisturising. This means that with a warming cleanser, you get all the skin care treatments in one product.

Some of the warming cleansers have Aloe Vera, antioxidants and vitamins that help to revitalize your skin. They are also a great idea for those who do not have the time or money to go to a salon or spa treatment to get facials.

These cleansers also work well for those who have blackheads and most of them are oil free and this makes them great for those with oily skin. Some warming cleansers have a medicinal scent while others have a fruity once. If you suffer from acne, warming cleansers will be a great benefit because they remove the oils and dirt that clogs the pores which is one of the causes of acne.

When you buy a warming cleanser, it is important to note that a little will go a long way therefore all you need is a small amount. Wet your face before using a warming cleanser and then dry your hands and put some of it on your palm. The cleanser should be massaged over the entire face and neck then rinsed out thoroughly. It is not advisable to use the product in the shower because it does not work well when it gets into contact with water. The **warming cleanser** begins heating up as soon as you start massaging it on your skin therefore you should be careful if you have sensitive skin. Unlike other cleansers that might lather on your skin, these warming cleansers do not lather. They spread evenly on your skin and feel thick and heavy but once you rinse if off, it leaves your skin clean. Your skin will not end up feeling squeaky when you use it because it does not remove any natural oils.

One of the **active ingredients in these warming cleansers is salicylic acid** which is one of the reasons why it works very well for those who suffer from acne and blackheads.

• • •

30

Acne and its Treatment

Acne is a common skin problem and people seek various forms of treatment to deal with it. One of the recent forms of treatment that has been developed is the exposed acne treatment. This treatment was developed by a group of naturopaths, chemists, dermatologists and cosmetologists. It makes use of the most effective medicines that are made available from nature and science to prevent and treat acne.

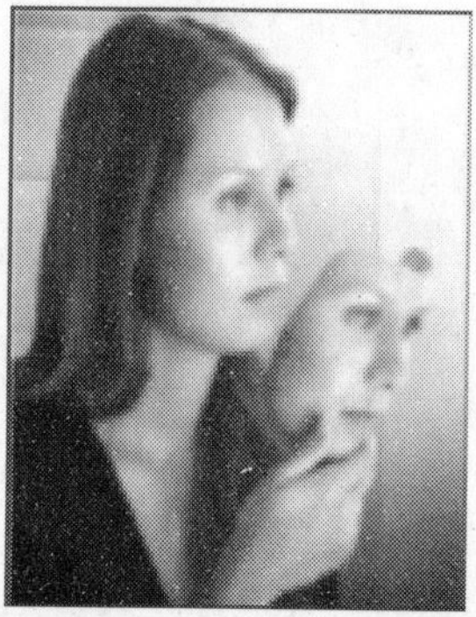

This treatment is one of a kind **skin care remedy** that will treat acne and prevent any new acne from forming on your skin. The difference between this treatment and other methods of treatment that are available is that no harsh medicines are used. The aim of the exposed acne treatment is to give your skin that healthy balance it once had. The exposed acne treatment clears any acne you have, prevents new breakouts, evens your skin tone and reduces the acne scars that you have.

The **treatment** has three steps that include:

1. Cleansing

The cleanser gets rid of dirt and any excess oil that your skin may have but will not affect the natural lipid layer. Any dead skin cells which may be clogging your pores will be cleared to allow the addictive that kills the bacteria that cause acne to penetrate into the skin pores.

2. Clearing

This step involves the use of a clearing tonic that has natural and manufactured additives that open the pores and remove dead skin cells. The tonic also removes both white and black-heads. The ingredients that are used help to soothe your skin and prepare it for the serum that will be used for the treatment.

3. Treating

This step uses a serum that is made of Micro-Benzoyl Peroxide which kills the bacteria that causes acne. The serum also helps to decrease the amount of sebum without drying your skin. The serum also has some natural addictives that are can help heal your skin if it is irritated.

There are a variety of active ingredients that are contained in the exposed **acne treatment**. First, there is **benzoyl peroxide** which is the active ingredients that kills the bacteria. This is the most important as once the bacteria are dealt with, acne is very easy to handle. The treatment also contains **Alpha Hydroxy Acid** which works well in getting rid of dead skin and the scars. The **Beta Hydroxy Acids** in the treatment will help to dry any acne that you have. This ingredient works on the pimples, zits, blackheads and cysts. The exposed acne treatment has green tea extracts that assist in controlling how much sebum your skin produces while clearing your skin at the same time. The olive leaf extracts will deal with any infection you may get and prevent the growth of bacteria. The tea tree oil that is used in the treatment helps your skin to heal and get proper nutrition. The other ingredients used in the treatment like **Aloe Vera**, and licorice sooth your skin and reduce aging.

• • •

31

Sun Protection

UV rays contribute to premature wrinkling, skin cancer and skin burning as well. In addition both kind of rays (UVA and UVB) can cause suppression of immune system in skin, which protect one from development and spread of skin cancer.

Adults and children should use sun protection daily. Most sunscreen products have a sun protection factor (SPF) rating on them. Generally, people with fair skin and light eyes need a strong sun protection factor. Sunscreen should be applied before going out in to the sun and reapply every two hours when working, playing or exercising outdoors. Protect your sun with a sunscreen that has an SPF of at least 15 or higher. Apply this product 30 minutes before sun exposure. Use waterproof sunscreen when swimming as the body will catch the sun. Reapply hourly to maintain adequate protection. Use a higher sun protection factor on the face, hands, arms and shoulders (if they're exposed) and lips can get sunburned, so you apply a lip balm containing a sunscreen with an SPF of 15 or higher.

When Sun Protection should begin?

Sun protection should begin as soon as a baby is born and continue throughout life. Babies should be kept out of direct sun light, especially those under six months old. Do not apply sunscreen to children under six month of old. Make sure children under six months of age wear a hat and are well protected from the sun's rays.

We now know that if a baby or child has a serious sun burn when they are young they are more prone to skin cancer when adults always protect your child by putting a sun block all over the exposed skin on his body and giving him a hat to wear which shades his face and neck. Sun block should be at least factor 20, which is specially designed for babies and children.

Minimize sun exposure, especially during the peak sun hours of 10 Am to 4 P.M., when solar radiation is most intense.

Wear appropriate clothing during prolonged periods in the sun-tight textile weave, long sleeves, pants and a full-brim hat.

• • •

32

Allergy Cause, Types and Treatment

The bodies defence mechanism works over time to react against foreign particles which may pose danger to normal functioning of the human system. These foreign particles are known as Allergens.

People who are known to be allergic, respond to harmless allergens in an exaggerated manner thus resulting in irritations and discomfort to the body.

There are several types of allergies like: Hay Fever, Asthma, Eczema, Hives, Contact Dermatitis (Skin Reactions), Conjunctivitis (Red eye), Sinusitis, Anaphylaxis (Life-Threatening Reaction).

For this general concept of the changed capacity for reaction, I propose the term "allergy". "Allo" denotes the deviation from the original state, from the behaviour of the normal, as in 'allorhythmia", "allotropy".

What are the Causes of Allergy?

Anything can act as an allergen if your system is sensitive to it, but the most common allergens are pollen, dust, dust mites, mold, mildew, cat and dog dander, foods (such as peanuts, milk and shellfish), drugs (such as penicillin and anesthetics) and certain chemicals.

What are the Symptoms of Allergy?

- A cold that never seems to go away. A running nose, congestion, or coughing that occurs pretty much constantly and lasts for more than 10 days can point to allergies.
- Symptoms have a pattern. Pollen allergies appear at the same time every year. Pet allergies happen when you are around a certain animal, or, in many cases, just enter a building where the animal lives. Dust allergies crop up when you clean house, shake out rugs or enter a very dusty building.
- Wheezing or frequent coughing could indicate a serious allergy or asthma.
- Coughing up mucus that is grey, yellow, green, brown, or bloody, or that is shaped like small strings or plugs.
- If eyes are persistently red and itchy.

How can we Diagnose Allergy?

Skin Tests

- The allergist injects extracts from allergens (such as dust mites, molds, or pollens commonly found in your area) into your skin to see whether your body has chemical substances to counteract the allergens from previous exposure. If you are sensitive to an allergen, a swollen rash will develop within 20 minutes after the test.
- Blood tests to determine how many white and red blood cells are there. Too many white cells might mean you have an infection in your system.

How can Allergy be Treated?

In general, it's best to start with small steps first -- avoiding allergens by getting rid of old rugs, for instance, and bathing the dog more often -- and then working your way up to the stronger antidotes like Anti-histamics or Decongestants, that stop the allergic reaction.

Desensitization to the allergens that bother you by taking a series of injections over a number of years. However, they are often reserved for people who have severe allergic symptoms (such as life-threatening allergies to stinging insects) that cannot be relieved by taking oral medications or avoiding allergens.

More Valuable information about Allergy...

People who get severe allergic reactions or anaphylaxis generally get them from insect stings, some medication, and food. More rarely, this severe reaction follows an allergy injection, after vigorous exercise or during anesthesia.

Whatever the cause, the body launches an emergency state of allergic reaction, flooding all systems with histamine and other chemicals. Capillaries and blood vessels expand (which explains the sensation of flushing and the dangerous drops in blood pressure, often described as feeling faint or going into shock), the bronchial tubes constrict (causing wheezing or difficulty in swallowing) and sometimes the throat and mouth swell, a dangerous symptom that can cause suffocation, coma and even death.

The early symptoms are usually quite noticeable, including a feeling of warmth or tingling in the skin and lips and an itchy rash, often between 10 seconds and 15 minutes after contact with the allergen. More extreme symptoms such as feeling lightheaded, dizzy, nauseated, having stomach cramps, hoarseness, difficulty in swallowing , breathing and a sense of panic follow rapidly. Lack of oxygen often turns the skin blue, too (a condition called cyanosis).

On Asthma: Not all people with asthma have allergies. Roughly 5 per cent of the population lives with asthma. A generally accepted definition of asthma is that, it is a disease that is characterized by increased responsiveness of the trachea (windpipe) and bronchi (main airway) to some type of trigger that causes widespread narrowing of the airways that changes in severity either as a result of treatment, or spontaneously.

Frequently asked questions about Allergy..

Which specialist should I consult if I have an allergic reaction?

You can see a General Physician or a Dermatologist.

Are Allergies Curable?

The body's reaction to allergens can be modified but cannot be completely removed.

Is it a Serious Problem?

Allergy can at times complicate into serious reactions (like Anaphylaxis), so one must take allergies seriously.

• • •

33

Boils / Skin Abscess General Information

A boil, or skin abscess, is a localized infection deep in the skin. A boil generally starts as a reddened, tender area. Over time, the area becomes firm and hard. Eventually, the centre of the abscess softens and becomes filled with white cells that the body sends to fight the infection. This collection of white cells is known as pus. Finally, the pus "forms a head" and drains out through the skin. Skin abscesses may occur anywhere on the body. They affect people of all ages.

There are several different types of boils. Among these are:

Furuncle or Carbuncle: This is an abscess in the skin caused by the bacteria Staphylococcus Aureus. It can have one or more openings onto the skin and may be associated with a fever or chills.

Cystic acne: This is a type of abscess formed when oil ducts become clogged and infected. Cystic acne is most common in the teenage years.

Hidradenitis Suppurativa: This is an illness in which there are multiple abscesses that form under the arm pits and in the groin area. These are a result of local inflammation of the sweat glands.

Pilonidal Cyst: This is a special kind of abscess that occurs in the crease of the buttocks. These frequently form after long trips that involve sitting.

Know Your Skin

What are the causes of Abscess?

There are many causes of boils. Some boils can be caused by an ingrown hair. Some are caused when a localized infection causes pus and infected material to collect in the skin or subcutaneous tissue. Others, such as those of acne, are caused by plugged sweat glands that become infected. Skin abscesses may follow a bacterial infection, commonly an infection with a bacteria called staphylococcus.

What are the Symptoms of Skin Abscess?

- Skin lesion maybe seen.
- Abscess will be in the form of open sore or closed, domed nodule.
- There maybe localized swelling, redness and induration.
- Affected area is tender and warm to touch.

How to Diagnose an Abscess?

The diagnosis is based on the appearance of the abscess.

Culture or examination of drainage from the lesion is done to find the causative organism.

How can Abscess be Treated?

Most simple boils can be treated at home. The main treatment for most boils is heat application, usually with hot soaks or hot packs. Heat may speed healing, reduce inflammation, and reduce discomfort.

Surgical incision and drainage of the abscess, with or without packing for 24 to 48 hours, cleans the area and allows infection to be controlled.

Antibiotics can be given

Complications of abscess are:

- Localized spread of infection.
- Impingement on the functioning of adjacent structures.
- Gangrene (tissue death).
- Systemic spread of infection will cause:
- Endocarditis.
- Osteomyelitis.
- Multiple new abscesses ("seeding" of infection).
- Abscess formation on the joints, pleura, or other locations.

Frequently asked questions about Abscess...

Which doctor should I consult for the treatment of skin abscess?

You can consult a General Physician.

Who is most likely to get a boil?

Anyone can get a boil. However, people with certain illnesses are more likely to develop boils. Among these illnesses are diabetes and kidney failure. Diseases that are associated with deficiencies in the normal immune system can increase the tendency to develop boils.

What can be done to prevent abscesses?

There are some measures that you can take to prevent abscesses from forming. Antibacterial soaps may help prevent bacteria build up on the skin and therefore reduce the chance for an abscess to form. In some cases, the doctor may recommend special cleansers to further reduce the bacteria on the skin.

Word Meaning

Abscess: Medical term for a common boil, a collection of pus beneath the skin.

Carbuncle: Painful localized bacterial infection. A circumscribed inflammation of the skin and deeper tissues that terminates in a slough and suppuration and is characterized by a painful node, at first covered by tight reddened skin which later becomes thin and perforates, discharging pus through several openings.

Furuncle: An acute circumscribed inflammation of the subcutaneous layers of the skin, gland or hair follicle.

Cyst: A closed sac or capsule, usually filled with fluid or semisolid material.

Antibiotic: A substance that inhibits the growth of or destroys bacteria or other microorganisms.

Pus: A thick whitish-yellow fluid which results from the accumulation of white blood cells (WBCs), liquified tissue and cellular debris. Pus is commonly a site of infection or foreign material in the body.

Gangrene: A necrosis, or death of tissue, usually due to deficient or absent blood supply.

Osteomyelitis: Inflammation of the bone due to infection, by the bacteria salmonella or staphylococcus.

Pleura: The thin covering that protects and cushions the lungs. The pleura is made up of two layers of tissue that are separated by a small amount of fluid.

• • •

34

Heat Stroke — Causes and Treatment

Heat stroke is the rise of body temperature following exposure to very high environmental temperatures. This could occur in hot weather, and in patients with pre-existing chronic diseases. If exposure to sun is the cause, then it is termed as sun stroke.

What are the Causes of Heat Stroke?

The factors pre-disposing to heat stroke are:

- Non-acclimatisation to high temperatures.
- Pre-existing illness with fever.
- High humidity.
- Obesity.
- Diabetes.
- Alcoholism.
- Ectodermal dysplasia (a birth defect with absence of sweat gland).
- Excessive muscular activity.
- Administration of sweat inhibiting drugs.

What are the Symptoms of Heat Stroke?

- The skin is hot and dry.
- The brain is affected resulting in restlessness, disorientation, delirium or even coma. Some milder

forms like headache, dizziness, and confusion are also seen.

- The rate of breathing is high and is usually shallow, intermittent or stertorous.
- Temperature within the mouth may increase beyond 108°F.
- Bleeding episodes from the nose may be present.
- The pulse may remain strong and rapid.
- The blood pressure is usually normal. A fall in blood pressure might indicate a more serious life-threatening situation called shock. This is a condition where there is reduced circulation of blood within the body, ultimately resulting in death.
- Cause of death can be due to, kidney failure, heart attack which is due to death of the heart muscle, heart failure due to the increase in work load on the heart or due to lung complications.

How can we Diagnose Heat Stroke?

After assessing the history and symptoms, the diagnosis becomes clear.

How can Heat Stroke be Treated?

This condition is an emergency. Rapid cooling of the body to a temperature of 102°F is required.

The patient is given ice water baths so as to bring down the body temperature. The patient's clothes have to be loosened so as to allow active air circulation. The body and the limbs have to be massaged in order to improve the blood circulation within the body.

Drugs to treat epileptic fits are administered, if the need arises. Blood transfusion if needed.

Shock is treated by supplying the body with sufficient fluids and by administering drugs, which increases the efficiency of the heart.

Prognosis is good in the face of prompt therapy. The risk factors are sudden onset of very high fever and shock.

Know Your Skin System

More Valuable information about Heat Stroke...

Heat syndromes are a group of six conditions, which occur on exposure to high environmental temperatures. They are:

- Heat Stroke.
- Heat exhaustion type 1.
- Heat exhaustion type 2.
- Water depletion heat exhaustion.
- Heat syncope.
- Heat cramps.

Heat exhaustion type 1: This is also called salt deficiency heat exhaustion. The condition occurs in prolonged sweating causing loss of salt from the body without sufficient replacement. The features are tiredness, nausea, vomiting, giddiness, cramps and dehydration. If untreated can lead to shock and circulatory failure.

Treatment is by bringing the salt-water ratio and blood volume back to normal.

Heat exhaustion type 2: This occurs after months of chronic exposure to hot and humid environment. The features are early tiredness, headaches, giddiness, boils on the dry areas of the skin seen around the arms and the trunk, increased heart rate, deep and fast breathing, and increase of body temperature to about 102°F.

Treatment is mainly to rest in a cool room. Ability to sweat improves the condition.

Heat syncope: This is also known as exercise induced heat exhaustion or heat collapse. This condition occurs in individuals unacclimatised to exposure to heat. It manifests as syncope, giddiness and tiredness. Recovery results in cool surroundings and after restoration of the salt-water balance in the body.

Water depletion heat exhaustion: This condition results in prolonged sweating followed by inadequate replacement of water. There is pronounced thirst, tiredness, reduced amount of urine production, fever, delirium and coma. A cool surrounding with adequate replacement of water helps the patient to recover.

Heat cramps: The development of painful muscular cramps in individuals with heavy sweating and salt depletion. Salt replacement helps to recover the patient from this condition.

Treatment: Immediate action necessary move to cooler place remove clothes apply cool packs, fan to increase air flow, transport to hospital.

Frequently asked questions about Heat Stroke...

- What are the precautions to be taken on a hot summer day?

The points to be remembered are:

1. Drink lot of fluids, like water and juices. Avoid carbonated, alcoholic or caffeine containing liquids.
2. Do not overexert yourself so as to increase the body's temperature to harmful levels.
3. Wear light coloured and slightly loose fitting clothes.
4. Try remaining in shaded areas to the extent possible.

35

Burns — Causes and Prevention

When a burn occurs to the skin, nerve endings are damaged causing the intense feelings of pain.

The infusion of large quantities of fluid, mainly a salt solution, as many as 3-4 litres daily, has proved satisfactory. Sometimes a life is saved if not more than one-quarter of the body surface has received a third-degree burn. In two cases blood transfusions to two patients with severe burns, with recovery in one case and postponement of death in the other.

Burn injuries, have reached epidemic proportions in recent years and are considered a health care problem that is more serious than the polio epidemic when it was at its peak. It has only been in the past several years that the medical profession has begun to recognize and understand the problems associated with burns. Burn accident statistics show that at least 50% of all burn accidents can be prevented. Across the world approximately 4.8 million burn injuries are reported per year. Between 18,000 and 22,000 patients with burns die, and approximately one million will sustain substantial or permanent disabilities resulting from their burn injury.

The kitchen is the most frequent area within the home where burn injuries occur for children newborn to four years in age. The second most frequent area in which burns occur is in the bathroom.

Burns can be of two kinds based on the extent of damage:

Partial Thickness Burns

In partial thickness burns, there may be redness due to capillary dilatation but the underlying germinal layer is intact.

Full Thickness Burns

In full thickness burns, the skin is completely destroyed.

What are the Symptoms of Burns?

Besides skin, burn injuries can affect muscles, bones, nerves, and blood vessels. The respiratory system can be damaged, with possible airway obstruction, respiratory failure and respiratory arrest. Burns impair the body's normal fluid/electrolyte (water and salt) balance, body temperature, body thermal regulation, joint function, manual dexterity. Patients may also suffer emotional and psychological problems.

What Causes the Burns and the Depth of Injury?

Thermal: including flame, radiation, or excessive heat from fire, steam, and hot liquids and hot objects.

Radiation: such as from nuclear sources. Ultraviolet light is also a source of radiation burns.

Light: burns caused by intense light sources or ultraviolet light, which includes sunlight.

Electrical: including electrical current and lightning.

Depth of Injury

First degree burns are superficial injuries that involve only the epidermis or outer layer of skin. They are the most common and the most minor of all burns. The skin is reddened and extremely painful. The burn will heal on its own without scarring within two to five days. There may be peeling of the skin and some temporary discoloration.

Second degree burns occur when the first layer of skin is burned through and the second layer, the dermal layer, is damaged but the burn does not pass through to underlying tissues. The skin appears moist and there will be deep intense pain, reddening, blisters and a mottled appearance to the skin. Second degree burns are considered minor if they involve less than 15 percent of the body surface in adults and less than 10 percent in children. When treated with reasonable care, second degree burns will heal themselves and produce very little scarring. Healing is usually complete within three weeks.

Third degree burns involve all the layers of the skin. They are referred to as full thickness burns and are the most serious of all burns. These are usually charred black and include areas that are dry and white. While a third-degree burn may be very painful, some patients feel little or no pain because the nerve endings have been destroyed. This type of burn may require skin grafting. As third degree burns heal, dense scars form.

First-Aid

- Remove patient from source of burn.
- Remove smoldering or contaminated clothes.
- Apply cold running water over the burnt area.
- Cover the victim with clean dry cloth or cling-film.
- Elevate the patient.

Know Your Skin

How can Burns be Treated?

- Local treatment in partial thickness wounds
- Cleaning
- Dressing with non-adherent paraffin gauze
- Medication in the form of cream
- Full thickness wounds

Immediate excision and skin grafting give good results in the long run. Donor skin may be taken from, other unaffected areas, from a relative, from skin banks or from the skin of pigs which are normally compatible with human skin (xenograft).

General Treatment

- Relieve pain with intravenous pain relievers or local anaesthetic creams
- Fluid replacement into the body to compensate the fluid loss
- Therapy to combat infection that can occur in the burnt area
- Anti-microbial therapy
- Nutritional support

More Valuable Information about Burns ...

Area burnt is calculated using the "Rule of Nine" where

¨Head and neck ¨1 × 9 = 9

¨Each arm ¨2 × 9 = 18

¨Each leg ¨2 × 9 = 18

¨Front of the trunk ¨2 × 9 = 18

¨Back of the trunk ¨2 × 9 = 18

¨Perineum ¨1

¨Patient's hand ¨1%

Complications Occurring at the Local Site

- Wound infection
- Scarring
- Wound contractures
- Complications occurring throughout the body
- Generalized Infection
- Acute peptic ulceration
- Seizures
- Kidney failure
- Psychological disturbance

Frequently asked questions about Burns...

Which specialist should I see if I have Burns?

You should immediately consult a general physician/ general surgeon.

What is the Prognosis of Burn Injury?

It can be roughly calculated by adding the patients age + percentage of body area having full thickness burns and if the total value exceeds 100, the patient's chance of survival is low.

Can Ink Help Burns?

No, always use cold water only.

• • •

36

Scabies and Pediculosis

Scabies

Scabies is a contagious disease caused by Sarcoptes scabei hominis, a tiny mite: male being 0.2 - 0.15 mm and female 0.4 - 0.3 mm in measurement. They are whitish hemispherical mites having 4 pairs of very short legs.

Clinical Features

The main complaint is itching which is worse at night. Incubation period is usually 2-3 weeks.

Skin lesions of scabies can be of three types:

- Lesions due to presence of mites are vesicles and burrows. Burrow is pathognomonic lesion which is 'S' shaped passage (5-15 mm), traversed by mite. It occurs most frequently on anterior aspect of wrists, the ulnar border of hand, interdigital webs, penis and palms and soles in infants. The vesicles are usually seen at the end of burrows.
- Lesions due to allergic sensitivity are small urticarial papules, excoriation marks and rarely inflammatory nodules, usually seen on lower abdomen, the buttocks, the thighs and the scrotum.

- Lesions due to complication can be pustular, impetiginous and eczematous. Rarely glomerulonephritis may complicate the pyoderma.

Other members of the family may also show similar manifestation. Sites of predilection are interdigital webs, the anterior aspect of wrist joint, the ulnar side of forearm, anterior fold of axillae, elbows, lower abdomen, penis and scrotum, arround the nipples in women and palms, soles and scalp in infants.

Disease is commonly seen in children but can affect any age. It usually spreads by intimate contact. Over crowding and poor hygiene also help in the spread of disease.

Treatment

Benzyl benzoate emulsion (25%), Gamma benzene hexachloride (1%), Monosulphiran (25%) and crotomiton (10%) are commonly used in treatment of scabies. In children, crotomiton (10%) and half strength of 25% benzyl benzoate emulsion should be used.

After a scrub bath, medicine is applied all over the body below neck. Next day again the patient is asked to apply the medicine without taking the bath and changing the clothes. On 3rd day patient is advised to take again a scrub bath followed by change of clothings. All the under garments and bed linen should be laundered or washed in boiling water.

A single treatment is sufficient but a second treatment should be advised only after an interval of 7 days, if re-examination discloses definite evidence of persistant infection. All the contacts should be treated at the same time to prevent cross infection. Antihistamines should be given to control itching. Secondarily, infected lesions should be treated with suitable antibiotics.

Norwegian Scabies

This form of scabies usually occurs in the mentally retarded and immunosuppressed. This is characterised by asymptomatic hyperkeratotic and crusted lesions usually present over trunk, limbs, palms and soles. Such cases are highly contagious.

Pediculosis

Pediculosis is an infestation caused by lice. There are three distinct types of lice according to the area infested:

(i) Pediculus humanus capitis (Head Louse)
(ii) Pediculus humanus corporis (Body Louse)
(iii) Phthirus pubis (Pubic Louse)

Pediculosis Capitis

P. capitis is caused by pediculus humanus capitis which is 3-4 mm in length and light brown in colour, usually prefers the scalp but may rarely live on beard and other hairy areas. It is transmitted by close contact or through combs or brushes. Poor personal hygiene is also an important predisposing factor. It is commonly seen in school children, especially those with long hair.

The patient complains of severe itching around the back and the sides of the scalp. Secondary bacterial infection, eczematisation and regional lymphadenopathy are common complications. The diagnosis can be confirmed by the demonstration of adult lice or by presence of small white nits (eggs) firmly attached to a hair shaft.

Treatment

It consists of application of 25% benzyl benzoate emulsion, 1% Gamma benzene hexachloride or 0.5% malathion on to the scalp hair. Next morning, the hair should be washed with a shampoo or soap. Nits may be removed with a special fine toothed comb. Treatment should be repeated after a week so as to kill the lice that may have hatched out of the nits. Secondary infections and eczematisation should be treated before specific therapy.

Pediculosis Corporis

Pediculosis corporis is caused by Pediculus humans corporis which is morphologically indistinguishable from head louse and its lives in the seams of the under clothes. It is commonly seen in individuals with grossly neglected poor hygiene and can be transmitted by close contact.

The patient will have severe itching with pinpoint macular or papular lesions, scratch marks, crusting and hyperpigmentation over the trunk and the shoulders.

Treatment

It consists of disinfection of clothes with 10% DDT 1% Gammabenzene hexa-chloride or 0.5% malathion. Clothings may also be sterilized by boiling or by use of a hot iron especially over the seams.

Pediculosis Pubis

It is caused by Phthirus pubis, which usually inhabits the anogenital area, the axillae, the eyelashes and the eyebrows. Infestation is often transmitted by sexual contact or through formites.

It causes intense itching and later secondary infection and eczematisation may occur. Bluish grey macule may be seen on the thighs, or lower abdomen. The nits are attached to the pubic hair or the hair of the regions mentioned.

Treatment

It is same as that of pediculosis capitis. Pediculosis of eyelashes can be treated by application of a one per cent ointment of yellow oxide of mercury.

• • •

37

Fungus Diseases

A fungus is a saprophytic or parasitic plant and is incapable of photosynthesizing its own organic food requirements due to lack of chlorophyll.

Despite the large number of fungi in the world, relatively few species of fungi are human pathogens. The fungi responsible for human disease may be either multicellular forming filaments known as hyphae or unicellular yeast which reproduce by budding. The fungal infections can be simply classified as follow:

1. Superficial mycoses, which affects skin and mucous membrane:
   - Dermatophyte infections (Tinea)
   - Candidiasis
   - Pityriasis versicolor
2. Deep mycoses, which invade the living tissue and causes systemic disease
   - Madura foot
   - Sporotrichosis
   - Chromomycosis

Superficial Mycoses

Dermatophyte Infections (Tinea)

These infections are caused by multicellular filamentous fungi, the dermatophytes, which invade the dead keratinized tissues i.e. the stratum corneum of skin, hair and nail. The dermatophytes are classified into three generas-microsporum, trichophyton and epidermophyton. Microsporum species produce disease in skin and hair, trichophyton in skin, hair and nail and epidermophyton in skin and nail.

Some of these dermatophytes live only on the humans, others primarily affect animals and a few dermatophytes thrive in the soil. Thus, dermatophyte infections may be transmitted to man from infected animal, man or soil. Poor nutrition and hygiene, a hot and humid climate, deblitating diseases, corticosteroid therapy and contact with infected animals, persons or fomites, all predispose to infection.

Dermatophyte infections are classified according to the anatomical sites of involvement. These clinical types and sites of infections are a follows:

- Tinea capitis (Scalp).
- Tinea barbae (Beard)
- Tinea corporis (Body)
- Tinea cruris (Groin)
- Tinea manuum (Hand)
- Tinea pedis (Foot)
- Tinea unguium (Nail)

Tinea Capitis

Tinea capitis is the fungal infection of the scalp caused by microsporum or trichophyton species. The disease mainly affects children and is usually contracted from infected combs or hair brushes. It is manifest in following types:

Grey patch type: This consist of single or multiple scaly, rough, grey patches from which most of the hair have fallen leaving a few broken stumps of lusterless hair. This type is commonly produced by T. violaceum, T. tonsurans and M. audouinii.

Black dot type: This is caused by T. violaceum. The affected hair break off at the scalp surface giving a 'black dot' appearance to the lesions.

Kerion: This is a painful inflammatory boggy swelling covering small or large area of the scalp in which hair are loose and fallout or can be easily epilated. This type of reaction is commonly caused by zoophilic dermatophytes like T. mentagrophytes and T. verrucosum. Follicular scarring and partial alopecia is common after severe kerion.

Favus: This is characterized by multiple, concave, yellowish crusts on fungal scalp, called 'scutula'. Each crust is composed of fungal filaments and epithelial debris and is pierced by a hair in the centre. This disease usually runs a chronic course and results in extensive cicatracial alopecia. It is commonly caused by T. schoenleinii.

Tinea Barbae

It occurs over the beard area of the face and neck T. mentagrophyte, T. verrucosum and T. violaceum are commonly responsible. Lesions may be of kerion type as seen in T. capitis, or superficial type of in which there are dry, rounded, red, scaly patches with short or brittle hairs.

Tinea Corporis

T. corporis is an infection of glaborous or nonhairy skin of the body, caused by species of Microsporum and Trichophyton. It is more commonly seen as itchy, red, circular scaly patches which clear centrally and slowly spread peripherally. The active border may show scales, populovesicles or pustules. Lesions may be single or multiple, discrete or coalesce to form polycyelic shapes.

Tinea Cruris

T. cruris is a fungal infection of the groin, thigh, perineum and perianal area E. floccosum, T. rubrum and T. mentagrophyte are the commonest causative agents. The lesions are usually bilaterally symmetrical, itchy, well defined, erythematous, scaly patches with active borders. The active borders, may be vesicular, pustular or scaly. Central clearance is often incomplete. Satellite lesion may be present.

Tinea Manuum

Tinea manuum is a fungal infection of hand commonly caused by T. rubrum. Clinically, it is characterised by diffuse, fine scaling and hyperkeratoses of the palm. Circumscribed vesicular patches of discrete red papular and follicular scaly patches may occur, especially on the dorsal aspect. Involvement is unilateral in most of the cases.

Tinea Pedis

T. pedis is a fungal infection of the dorsum of foot, sole and interdigital spaces. T. mentagrophyte, T. rubrum and E. floccosum are the usual causative fungi. It is more commonly seen in adult males, particularly those who wear socks and shoes constantly. The infection is also transmitted via infected bathroom floors and swimming baths. There are three main clinical variants:

- Interterigo type, characterised by scaly soddened whitish skin particularly in the space between 4th and 5th toes.
- Vesicular type, characterised by vesicular eruptions over instep portion of the sole, toes or dorsum of the

foot. The vesicles may become pustules. The lesions rupture and then dry leaving irregular collarette of scales. It is often associated with eruption of hands. T. metagrophyte is the most common fungus isolated from such lesions.

- Squamous hyperkeratotic type, characterized by scaly hyperkeratotic lesions on the sole and sides of the foot which may be patchy or diffuse. T. rubrum is common causative agent.

Tinea Unguium

T. unguium is a fungal infection of nails usually caused by T. rubrum. Toe nails are much more frequently involved than finger nails. The infection is ordinarily limited to one or more but rarely all of the nails. It involves the soft keratin of the nail bed and later extend upward into the hard keratin of the nail plate. The infection usually begins at the lateral or distal edges of the nail causing the nail to be discoloured, thickened and distorted. The distal portion of the nail plate separates from the nail bed due to accumulation of soft keratin debris underneath.

Diagnosis of Tinea Infections

KOH Preparation

Skin scrappings from the active edge of the lesions, nail clippings with subungual debris, or plucked hair are placed in a drop of 10-20% KOH solution on a microscopic slide, covered with a coverslip and heated gently to clear the keratin and then examined under microscope for presence of spores and hyphae.

Culture

The infected material (scales, hair, nail-clippings) may be cultured on sabouraud's-dextrose-agar media for identification of species.

Wood's Lamp

Infected hair are examined under wood's light for any fluorescence. The fungi which give fluorescence are M. canis, M. audouinii and T. schoenleinii.

Treatment of Tinea Infections

All tinea infections should be treated with topical antifungal agents and only supplemented by systemic therapy when the dermatophyte has invaded scalp, hairs or a large area of skin. Various topical anti-fungal agents like whitfield's ointment, Casellani's paint, clotrimazole, miconazole, econazole, have been used for treatment of dermatophyte infections. Topical agent is to be applied twice daily usually for about a month and to be continued for at least 7-10 days after the lesions have disappeared completely.

Griseofulvin and Ketoconazole are the two drugs available for systemic therapy. griseofulvin is given orally in the dosage of 250 mg twice a day after meals. Duration of treatment depends upon the clinical types of dermatophyte infection. T. capitis and T. pedis usually require 4 to 8 weeks therapy while T. unguium requires treatment for 4 to 8 months. Treatment of toe nail is often unsatisfactory.

Ketoconazole is a new broad-spectrum antifungal agent which is usually recommended in cases of Griseofulvin resistance and is given in dose of 200-400 mg/day with food.

General measures include personal cleanliness, thorough drying after washing, use of clean linens and avoidance of tight fitting shoes and undergarments.

Candidiasis

Candidiasis is an infection of skin, mucous membrane and visceras, caused by candida albicans or occassionally other candida species. Candida albicans is a normal inhabitant of oral cavity, gastrointestinal tract and vaginal mucosa. It can produce disease under certain favourable conditions like trauma and maceration, antibiotics and steroid therapy, diabetes mellitus, blood dyscrasias, pregnancy, malignancies and malnutrition.

Clinical Features

Mucosal candidiasis produces soft white plaques on the tongue and buccal surfaces which can be scrapped off to leave a bright red moist base. Similar lesions may occur on the mucosa of the vagina and usually associated with creamy discharge and marked local pruritis. Infection of the angle of the mouth may cause fissures (angular stomatitis). In male, glans penis and prepuce may show erythema and maceration (Balanoposthitis) though sexual contact with infected females.

Cutaneous candidiasis is characterized by moist, red macerated areas with poorly defined margins and satellite vesico-pustules. Pruritis is usually present and at times may be intense. It typically involves the body folds, the napkin area in infants or the nail folds.

Diagnosis

Demonstration of candida, especially in mycelia form in KOH preparation confirms the diagnosis. Culture can be done on Sabouraud's-dextrose-agar media.

Treatment

Various topical agents such as gentian violet 1%, haymycin, nystatin, miconazole and clotrimazole are highly effective in the treatment of candidal infection. For oral candidiasis, nystatin suspension is kept in the mouth for few minutes and then swallowed. In vulvo-vaginitis, nystatin, clotrimazole or miconazole pessaries are inserted twice daily for 2 weeks and it is advisable to give oral nystatin to prevent the recurrences.

In every patient, underlying predisposing factors should be corrected as far as possible.

Pityriasis Versicolor

Pityriasis Versicolor is a mild, chronic, asymptomatic infection of the most superficial layers of the skin caused by Pityrosporum orbiculare. It is very common in warm and humid climate and usually affect young adults. It is characterized by fine, scaly, hyper or hypopigmented macules of varying sizes and shapes which appear on trunk, upper arms, shoulders and neck. Macules may become confluent to form polycyclic patches.

Diagnosis

The microscopic examination of skin scrapping in a KOH preparation reveals short hyphae and cluster of round and budding, yeast cells. Scaly lesions usually show golden yellow fluorescence when examined under wood's light.

Treatment

Selenium sulphide shampoo (2.5%) is applied to the affected part at bed time and washed off next morning. Such treatment is being repeated after 5-7 days. Miconazole or clotrimazole are also effective and applied twice daily for 10-14 days. Oral ketoconazole (200-400 mg/ day) may be used in cases with extensive and long standing eruptions.

Madura Foot (Mycetoma)

Mycetoma is a chronic granulomatous condition which affects skin, subcutaneous tissue and bones. It may be Eumycetoma, caused by variety of fungi (madurella mycetoma and Madurella grisea) or Actinomycetoma, caused by aerobic actinomycetes (Nocardia and Actinomedura medurae). The disease is common in adult males and usually occurs after trauma. The commonest site is the foot or hand but other sites may be involved.

Clinically, it is characterized by presence of firm to hard subcutaneous nodules and swellings. These nodules break open and discharge pus containing grains. There may be involvement of underlying bones and joints by the invasion of the fungus.

Diagnosis

It is made by microscopic examination of the grains from the lesion and culture of the fungi.

Treatment

Treatment of eumycetoma is usually unsatisfactory but amphotericin B and griseofulvin may be tried. In actinomycetoma, combination of dapsone with streptomycin or cotrimoxazole plus streptomycin has been reported to give good results.

In some cases, medical therapy may have to be supplemented by surgical excision, drainage and curettage of sinuses.

Sporotrichosis

It is a chronic infection of skin, subcutaneous tissue and lymph nodes, caused by Sporothrix schenckii. The lesions are usually initiated by trauma inoculating organism into subcutaneous tissue and are found mainly in farmers.

Clinically, it is characterized by presence of nodulo-ulcerative lesions in a linear fashion along the lymphatics. Regional lymphnodes may be enlarged. Rarely, sporotrichosis may disseminate via the blood stream. The diagnosis is made by histology and culture of biopsy material.

Treatment

The condition respond to oral saturated potassium iodide solution, starting with 5 to 10 drops and gradually increased to 15 drops, three times a day. Intravenous miconazole and oral ketaconazole have also been used with some success.

Chromomycosis

It is a cutaneous and subcutaneous mycosis caused by species of phialophora and cladosporium. Adult male agriculture workers are most often affected. The organism enters the skin after trauma.

Clinically, it is characterized by the development of multiple, indurated papulo-nodules on the foot or leg which slowly increase and take verrucous cauliflower like appearance. These lesions may ulcerate and later become secondarily infected. New crops of satellite lesions are usually seen along the path of lymphatic drainage.

Diagnosis

It is confirmed by culture or demonstration of clusters of brownish spores in biopsy material or in KOH preparation.

Treatment

Surgical excision or cryotherapy is the treatment of choice for small lesions. Systemic ketoconazole, amphotericin B or 5-fluorouracil may also be effective.

• • •

38

Urticaria

Urticaria is a common vascular reaction pattern characterized by dermal swelling due to vasodilatation and increased vascular permeability. Clinically, it is manifested as intensely itchy, erythematous or pale, oedematous swelling.

Mechanism

It is mainly due to lical increase of permeability of the capillaries and the small venules. Histamine, which is derived from mast cell, is an important mediator. Kinins, prostaglandins, fibrinolysin system and complements are other important mediators.

Urticaria can be produced by wide variety of immunological and non-immunological (Physical, chemical, drugs) stimuli.

Provoking Causes

- Aero-allergens
- Blood products and bites (insects)
- Contactants
- Drugs
- Endogenons disease
- Foods
- Genetic diseases

- Physical urticaria
- Infections/Infestations and Idiopathic

Aero-allergens

Important aero-allergens are pollens, housedust, feathers, spores etc.

Blood Products and Insect Bites

Urticaria can be seen with blood transfusion. Bites or stings due to spiders, snakes, insects can produce urticaria by immunological as well as by non-immunological mechanism.

Contactants

Wide variety of contactants like drugs, dyes, cosmetics, tooth paste, fabrics, soaps etc. can be responsible for urticaria.

Drugs

Drugs can produce urticaria by immunological as well as by non-immunological mechanism. The common drugs are penicillamine, sulfonamides, coedine, aspirin and other anti-inflammatory agents, insulin, morphine, thyroid and parathyroid extracts.

Endogenous Diseases

This includes lupus erythematosus, malignancies, polycythemia, psycological factors and endocrinal disorders.

Food

Food allergy usually results in acute or recurrent attacks or urticaria, starting with in minutes or few hours of ingestion and lasting for few hours/days. Common foods are: nuts, fish, eggs, chocolate, tomato, milk, cheese etc. Preservatives and dyes in food are other important factors.

Genetic Diseases

It includes heriditary angioderma and familial cold urticaria.

Physical Urticaria

It is a distinct group in which localised oedema occur in response to physical stimuli i.e. cold, heat, solar rays, pressure, vibrations and water. Dermographism is a type of physical urticaria in which firm stroking of skin causes an exaggeration to triple response (erythema, oedema, and flare).

Infections/Infestations

Urticaria has been seen with viral, bacterial, fungal and parasitic infections. Mechanism is believed to be immunological.

Treatment

It is essential to take very careful and detailed history and make a thorough physical examination to detect the cause. If cause is found, avoidance of that causative agent is obviously the treatment of choice. However, due to difficulty in identifying or eliminating such a factor, symptomatic treatment should be given. Antihistamine drugs are the mainstay in the management of urticaria. The combination of H_1 and H_2 blocker (Cimetidine) may be effective in treatment of chronic urticaria. The tricyclic antidepressant (Doxipin) adrenergic agonist (Terbutaline) may be beneficial in a few cases. Systemic steroids are only inidcated in very acute or recalcitrant cases.

Angio Oedema

This is a variant of urticaria in which subcutaneous tissue rather than dermis is mainly involved. It commonly affects the lips, periorbital tissues, genetalia and sometime even tongue and larynx. Itching is usually absent.

Treatment is same as that of chronic urticaria. Acute cases require abrenaline and corticosteroids.

• • •

39

Skin Cancer

Skin cancer is the third most common cancer occurring in women in the 15-34 year-old age group. If you notice any changes in the size or shape of moles on your skin, itching or bleeding, you should see a specialist as quickly as possible. A common site for skin cancer in women is on the legs. With men, it is often found on the back.

With early detectin, skin cancer is curable. Be aware and take preventative measures to-avoid burning and always cover up with a high protection sunscreen. Sunscreen worn on a daily basis, is the single fastest way to protect the health and appearance of your skin, both now and for the future.

Photosensitization

The skin can react to plant and fruit extracts and juices (figs in particular), drugs or chemicals when exposed to the sun, resulting in a sore, itchy red rash or blisters.

Soothe with cold compresses, showers and calamine lotion.

If you are going to sunbathe, avoid using perfume, aftershave, anti-bacterial soaps, artificial sweeteners, medications containing diuretics or tranquillizers.

Polymorphic Light Eruption (PLE)

This is a common condition whereby the skin is abnormally sensitive to sunlight. It usually starts in the spring when sunlight becomes stronger and lasts throughout the summer causing itching, redness and a variety of rashes. It is thought that UVA plays a particular role in PLE and one clinical trial reported good results when sufferers used a sunscreen with very high levels of UVA protection.

Functions of the Skin

- Provides a protective barrier between the environment and the body.
- Shields internal organs from injury, sunlight and germs.
- Sensory organ-it is sensitive to touch, pain and temperature.
- Keeps body temperature constant.
- Provides a waterproof barrier.
- Serves to maintain the balance of body fluids.
- Organ for elimination of fluids, minerals and other biochemicals.

Home Skin-Care Programme

Your kitchen can offer many possibilities for natural skincare.

Avocado

Rich in mono-unsaturated oils, avocados make a healthy addition to the diet from outside and the inside. To make a rich after shampoo conditioner, mash together one ripe avocado, some honey and a little avocado or olive oil. Spread thickly on the hair and rinse off after 5 or 10 minutes.

Cucumber

Use slices of cucumber to pep up tired eyes, or grate a quarter of a cucumber, squeeze it to extract the juice and mix it with a cupful of milk. Use the mixture with cotton wool as a cleanser - ideal for normal to oily skin. Cucumber juice also makes a cooling addition to your basic skin cream.

Milk

Soothe away tension in a warm, moisturising bath with added milk–perhaps not as many tons of asses milk as Cleopatra used, but a cup or two of silver top will yield almost identical benefit.

Oats

A staple food of the scots and recently in vogue for its high content of soluble fibres, which may have cholesterol-lowering effects. Oats can also be made into a useful body scrub. Make a gentle scrub by mixing oats with honey, yoghurt and ground almonds into a paste–good enough to eat.

Water

Drink as much pure and fresh water as you can. It will cleanse your skin from the inside out. Or spray a fine mist of water over your face before moisturising to seal in the moisture and retain a youthful look.

Yoghurt

Egyptian women have used it for thousands of years as a cleanser and beauty aid. Live yoghurt contains bacteria which, in turn, kill the bacteria that may contribute to spots and blemishes. Apply natural yoghurt to the face and skin, relax and leave it on for 5 to 10 minutes before rinsing it off and moisturising.

• • •

40

Marks and Spots on the Face and Leucoderma

Any kind of spot or a number of spots on the face spoil the personality charm of a woman. Every beauty-conscious woman wants to avoid such beauty-deterrents. The spots are of various kinds like dark spots beneath the eyes, white patches and small-pox spots. The dark rings below the eyes make a woman look older than her age. In this jet-set world of today about ninety percent of women suffer from various kinds of tensions which have maximum affect on skin and eyes. Eyes keep sinking everyday and are surrounded by dark circles. Wrinkles appear on them. This blackishness and wrinkles are not confined to eyes only but spread over the entire face making a person look old even in young age.

Now you may question as to why these dark spots and wrinkles appear first around eyes only? The reason is that the skin around eyes is very sensitive and contains a very thin layer of fat. If this fat remains healthy then the eyes do not sink. When the fat gets reduced and becomes dead there is little or no flow of blood in it and the veins cannot hold the eyes at the initial level.

Although, make-up helps in hiding these dark spots to a certain extent, it is necessary to control the psychological factors, so as to cure these permanently. Avoid tensions, increase the intake of vitamin 'C', and consult your physician to check the internal disorders, if any. Green vegetables, lemon and orange are very rich in vitamin 'C', which purify blood-carrying veins in the body and maintain the natural glow of skin. Women should apply only that much make-up which looks natural to their personality. It is necessary to clean every trace of make-up at night otherwise the pores on the skin get blocked and their activity is stopped. Thus body-waste remain inside and their rotting process makes the skin unattractive.

Do not rub the area around the eyes, because rubbing may result in shrinking of the skin. Use the middle finger of left hand and tap lightly. The skin around the eyes remains healthy by putting a mixture of rose water and cucumber juice in the eyes. You may use anti-wrinkle cream or hormone cream in case of wrinkles or dark spots around your eyes. Following is a home-made remedy for it:

Boil tea-leaves and strain, foment the area below eyes with this warm decoction.

A light massage by applying almond oil on the skin at night is beneficial. Massage should always be with outward strokes towards temples.

Another home-made method for removing shadows is as below:

Wrap oat flour and dust of sandalwood in a napkin. Soak it in unheated milk or rose water and rub on the face.

Pock-Marks

A pock-marked face is a curse. Make-up can hide these marks but cannot remove them. There are two ways to remove them permanently:

- Sand-paper surgery
- Skin-peeling

Sand-paper surgery is generally done in foreign countries. It is not prevalent in India due to its exhorbitant cost. The patient has to suffer a lot of pain due to numerous small operations on the skin. These operations should be done only by a specialist. For skin-peeling, many kinds of pastes are appeeled off after application of every paste. The skin gets spotless after repeating the process many times.

Small-pox spots get reduced with the advancement of age from childhood to adolescence and the growth of body. Women must look after their skin, specially their face. At night, before sleeping use deep cleansing-milk and apply nourishing cream. Facials also reduce these spots. Lanolin cream, which is available in market, also helps in eliminating them. Soyabean paste fills the deep spots. Apply soyabean paste on face. Let it dry for fifteen to twenty minutes, then wash it with lukewarm water. This process must be repeated thrice a week.

White Spots [Leucoderma]

To have white spots or patches on the body is a disease. It is known as leucoderma. This is not a contagious disease. Imbalance of melanin in the body results in appearance of white spots. These white patches are a curse for women. These patches are directly related to the nature of the skin. Darker skins have more patches because such skin carry more melanins. It must be clarified here that white patches are not congenital nor hereditary. Children are not affected if the mother has these patches. It is erroneous to think that a woman having leucoderma, suffers from enjoying marital pleasures. Generally, doctors recommend a solution of carbolic acid to be applied around the spots to

prevent them from spreading. Ayurvedic medical science practitio-ners recommend bawachi oil massage and in many cases the repeated massaging brings the skin to its normal colouring. Natural therapy can also be used as a remedial measure but it is too costly to be popular in India. Make-up helps in hiding these spots temporarily. Apply 'foundation' after thoroughly cleaning the skin, the colour of the 'foundation' should be darker than the colour of your skin. Now apply face powder and apply make-up as per your wish. At night it is useful to apply calamine lotion after removing the make-up completely. The spots and the rest of the normal skin should be massaged with calamine lotion. Try homoeopathic medicines by consulting a homoeopathic physician.

41

Hair — its Structure Growth and Colour

Good looking hair is essentially healthy, shiny and clean. But our hair is constantly exposed to the aggressions of the environment and age and these tend to have a negative influence on its appearance–so most of the hair-care products we use, aim at reducing these effects thereby making the hair look attractive as our crowning glory.

Structure of Hair

Hair is all protein: The part of the hair we see is dead; the actual living part is very small and is at the root in a part known as the papilla. In the papilla, cells multiply and produce a protein called hard keratin - this is responsible for the hardness of the hair.

The part of the hair which is within the skin, is enclosed by a sleeve of tissue called the follicle. Next to each follicle is a sebaceous gland, the oil producing factory of the skin. This oil forms a natural protective film over the length of hair, keeping it soft, shiny and supple.

Each hair is made up of three layers: the cuticle or the outer most layer which has tiny overlapping transparent scales. When the scales lie flat against each other, the hair appears shiny, but when the scales are lifted, hair seems rough and dull. Conditioning rinses help to keep the scales positioned correctly, giving it a smooth and shiny appearance.

The cuticle of the hair is selectively porous. This porosity varies along the length of the hair, the youngest bit near the scalp being the least porous. Also oily hair is less porous than dry hair. The porous nature of hair allows for the penetration of chemicals. The agents used in bleaches, tints and perms capitalise on this nature of the hair-the chemicals used are quickly absorbed and bring about the necessary changes in colour and curliness.

The cortex or middle layer of hair contains the colour pigment granules. The colour of hair depends on the number, size and distribution of the pigment granules in the cortex and also on the nature of pigment present. Colourants and bleaches work by penetrating the cuticle so that the colour is added to or subtracted from the cortex. The innermost layer is the medulla; it is absent in very fine hair.

Shape And Colour of Hair

Straight hair or curly hair?

Curly hair has a flattened cross-section while straight hair has a circular one. The basic hair form is controlled by a number of genes-but this hair form is readily altered by chemicals present in perming and straightening lotions.

Thick hair or fine hair?

Except for palms, soles and lips, hair is present all over the body. In some areas it is long, thick and dark-this is the terminal hair seen on the scalp, on the face of adult men and in the axilla and pubic region of adults; some terminal hair are also present on the arms, legs and body. The hair on the rest of the skin is short, fine, light, and inconspicuous: this type of hair is called the vellus hair.

Sometimes hair which is normally supposed to be fine and inconspicuous becomes visible; for instance terminal hair appears on the face of women in a condition called hirsutism. On the other hand, sometimes terminal hair gets converted into fine vellus hair-this happens in the all familiar baldness seen in men.

Colour of your hair

The colour of your hair depends on the number, size and distribution of pigment granules in the cortex and the nature of the pigment present. The granules in black, blonde and red hair are different chemically: the brown black hair is due to melanin, the blonde hair contains phaeomelanin and red hair erythromelanin.

It is thought that a number of genes influence of the colour of the hair-some of these genes also influence other inherited characteristics as well: the association between hair colour and hair form is well established. There is also an obvious association between hair colour and the colour of the eyes, the colour of the skin and the presence of freckles.

Though, the basic colour of your hair is determined by your genes, this colour is readily altered by colouring agents. It can be lightened using bleaches, highlighted by a variety of agents and darkened by several types of natural and synthetic hairdyes.

Hair Growth

How fast does hair grow?

The rate of hair growth varies considerably but on an average it is one cm per month. The growth is greater in summer than in winter. It is maximum in the ages between 15-30 years. Cutting or shaving does not make hair grow faster. Neither does trimming affect the growth rate in any way (though trimming does make your hair look good by eliminating the straggly ends.

Each hair undergoes cyclic activity in three phases: the growth phase or anagen lasts for 3-4 years; following anagen is a short period of transition or catagen, following which is the phase of telogen or resting. During the resting phase (2-3 months) the hair becomes detached from its root and falls out, as a new growing hair replaces it in the follicle.

At a given time, 10-15% of the scalp hair are in an inactive phase, ready to fall out, while the remaining are in various stages of growth. A loss of up to 100 hairs per day is normal and is something you should not worry about as most of the lost hair would be replaced. With age, however, the rate of replacement slows down; so as you grow older, there is a natural tendency of some amount of sparseness of your scalp hair.

What controls the growth of hair?

- Family background and racial factors are very important for the quality as well as the quantity of hair. Good quality long hair runs in families, and so does the all familiar male type of baldness.
- **Nutrition:** Hair like any other aspect of your looks is best improved by treating your system well. A good balanced diet is what is really required. An inadequate diet disturbs the structure, the growth and the colour of hair. When there is a total deficiency of protein, the hair becomes sparse, fine, brittle, dry and light coloured. The severe hair loss seen after crash diets is primarily due to protein deficiency. High protein diets especially those containing gelatin and cysteine have been seen to have increased the rates of hair growth. Deficiency of pantothenic acid

leads to premature graying of hair in animals. Lack of essential fatty acids also causes hair to fall. Iron deficiency, especially in women, has been associated with hair loss, while iron supplementation hastens the growth of hair. Zinc deficiency also leads to hair fall. So an ideal diet for hair growth should contain adequate amounts of iron, protein and fatty acids.

- **Age :** With progressively increasing age, there is a decrease in hair growth. The replacement of shed hair is also incomplete and this results in sparsity of hair. In men, there is a recession of the hairline and sometimes definite areas of baldness appear. This baldness is dependent on the male sex hormones–the androgens. Rarely this hormone-mediated baldness is seen in women too.
- **Hormones:** A number of other hormonal disorders can cause hair loss-thyroid disorders being the commonest. Though during pregnancy, hair loss slows down or may even stop altogether, excessive hair fall commonly occurs three to four months after delivery. Contraceptive pills also cause excessive hair loss and this stops when the pill is discontinued.

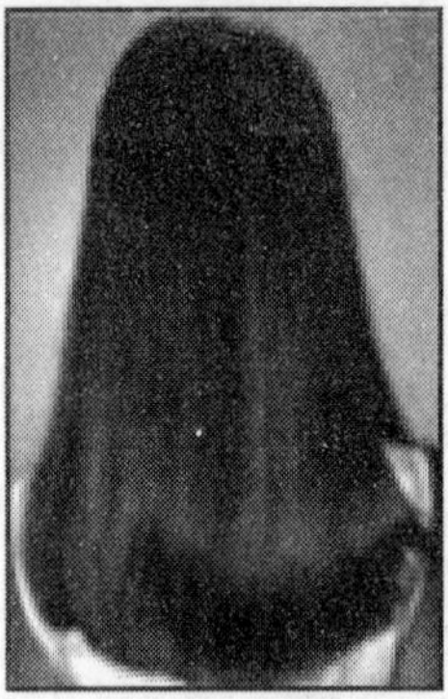

• • •

42

Normal Care for your Hair

Here are some questions and answers for normal care of your hair.

Which is Better-Combing or Brushing?

If you use a soft brush, brushing is less damaging then combing, but a stiff brush does cause more damage to the hair than a comb. Prolonged brushing also harms the hair considerably. So the proverbial 100 strokes a night may actually harm the hair. Back-combing also damages the hair. It ruffles the scales of the cuticle as well as it causes knotting which is difficult to untangle.

Wet hair should never be combed or brushed because hair sticks together when wet and a greater force is required to comb or brush it and this causes greater damage to the hair. Moreover, the bonds (hydrogen bonds) which are responsible for the strength of the hair are broken temporarily when the hair is wet. This makes wet hair weak and more likely to be broken by combing or brushing.

A good comb should have rounded and not sharp teeth. Brush ends should also always be rounded to minimise mechanical damage to the hair. Nylon brushes with spiky ends also damage the hair. The best hair brushes are made of bristles from the hair of wild boar the tiny scales on the bristles clean the hair and give it a sheen.

How to Choose your Shampoo?

The aim of shampoos is not only to clean the hair, but to beautify it as well. Most shampoos are detergent based. To this are added several chemicals-stabilisers, preservatives, conditioning agents, perfumes and colours.

A shampoo should be judged by its performance–not by its appearance, colour, perfume and definitely not by its price. It should clean the hair and rinse out easily, leaving the hair smooth and manageable. Lots of lather is not a measure of its efficiency–though it may indicate a high detergent content. Neither does a thick consistency mean that the shampoo is more concentrated.

There is a good range of products–labelled as 'for oily hair', 'for dry hair', and 'for normal hair'. The differences between these shampoos is in the type of the detergent used and also in the concentration of the detergent used. Shampoos with high detergent activity are based on anionic surfactants and those claiming mildness generally contain non-ionic surfactants. Scientific studies have shown almost identical efficiencies for various shampoos, whether designated for oily or dry hair. All shampoos do leave behind a constant residue of oil because this is beyond the reach of surfactant–this is nature's way of protecting the hair fibres from injuries.

Regarding the pH of shampoos, it is generally agreed that neutral or slightly acidic shampoos are better for the hair, especially the hair that has been physically or chemically damaged. This is because the acids precipitate proteins on the hair surface which acts as a protective coat for the damaged hair.

How safe are Shampoos?

Shampoos are very safe for the hair because they do not contain any harsh detergents, therefore the natural coating, the hydrolipidic film, is retained on the hair. Excessive cleansing, may sometimes give rise to a 'flyway condition' of the hair. The hair then becomes unmanageable due to 'static' build up. The main problem, with shampooing, however, is the mechanical abrasion of wet hair caused by rubbing movements while shampooing and by towel drying. Reactions to shampoos are infrequent; the main problem is the irritation of eyes but the newer detergents and chemicals in baby shampoos are free even from this problem.

How often Should you Wash your Hair?

This depends on the type of hair and scalp, and also on the environment. If your hair is greasy then you would need to wash it frequently, say even 3-4 times every week. This is especially necessary, if the environment you work in is dirty. Frequent shampooing is not harmful for the hair.

Do exotic shampoo ingredients have any real effect on the hair?

Despite their popularity and appeal, many of the shampoo additives do not really benefit the hair, simply because they are quickly rinsed off the hair in the shampooing process. However some products, egg and beer for instance, may cling to the hair and impart apparent body to the hair and act as conditioning agents.

Some shampoos contain exotic, natural additives like– collagen, gelatin, allantoin, and henna. Gelatin, which is nothing but the simplest of collagens, is almost ineffective. Broken down gelatin gives additional body and softness to the hair. Experiments have shown that it may be possible to even repair split ends, under optimal pH conditions, with hydrolysed gelatin. Amino acids and panthenol are added to some shampoos because they give body to the hair. Henna is another ingredient being used in more and more shampoos. The extract which is added is colourless and gives body and gloss to the hair without any colouration.

How do Conditioners Work?

There is nothing long lasting about the effect of conditioners but they definitely do have a temporary magical effect on the hair.

Degradative changes of the hair are caused by combing, brushing, washing and drying. The scales of the hair cuticle are damaged–these then curl up and break. Since smooth overlapping scales are essential for shiny hair, the damaged hair appears dull and lifeless.

Conditioners do not penetrate the outer layer of the hair shaft–they merely coat the hair, helping to flatten and smoothen scales. A fine fatty film is deposited on the hair shaft; this temporarily fills in broken patches in the cuticle, just like plaster does over cracks in the wall. This softens the hair and gives it shine and body. Conditioners also restore the protective acidic film which is reduced during shampooing.

Hair is 'electrically changed' immediately after shampooing. So it easily tangles and becomes difficult to manage. The active ingredient of most creme-rinse conditioners is a cationic surfactant. This reduces the friction between hair bibres and increases surface conductivity, so the electric change is lost and hair becomes manageable.

Which Conditioner to Choose?

Conditioners are generally used after shampooing. Creme-rinses are kneaded into the wet hair immediately after rinsing off the shampoo. The hair is then rinsed thoroughly after 1 to 2 minutes. If the conditioner is not rinsed off well, the hair may appear greasy.

Sometimes the conditioning agents are incorporated into shampoos; the conditioning performance of such combination shampoos is inferior to the performance of the 2-stage shampooing and conditioning. Newer conditioning agents have, however, been added to shampoos without loss of the conditioning effects.

The term 'balsam' is frequently mentioned in connection with creme-rinses. The term is applied to conditioners which contain plenty of oils and protein. Exotic natural additives such as collagen, gelatin, allantoin and henna are also being used in the conditioners. Some of these have questionable effect while others add to the body and shine of the hair.

Are Conditioners Safe?

The conditioning compounds are not without adverse effects. The hair may be softened too much–this happens frequently with thin hair. A major problem with cationic agents is that they are highly irritating to the eyes and many cause defective vision due to the development of cataracts. As this happens with higher concentrations of the conditioning chemicals, their levels should be strictly controlled.

How Made Rinses for your Hair?

Lime juice, vinegar and tea water are often quoted as good hair rinses: They, in fact, do not offer the benefits of the easily available commercial conditioners. In the days when people used soap to wash their hair, a dull covering formed over the hair in the presence of hard water. All the above being acids, helped remove the soap scum. Nowadays this quality is of no value as the detergents used in modern shampoos do not precipitate with hard water. However, since most shampoos are alkaline, these acids do neutralise the residual effects of the shampoos and may form an acidic coating on the hair.

Injured Hair

What is the Cause of Split Ends?

If it is not cut, the hair can grow to a length of 40 to 80 cms. During its long stay on the scalp, the hair is exposed to innumerable physical and chemical traumas: combing and brushing, shampooing, weathering and chemical treatments. These factors are all the more damaging to hair because hair is a dead structure that lack the power of self-repair. The cumulative effect of all these injuries is the gradual wearing down of the cuticle scales–these are totally lost at the tips of the hair and this results in split ends.

What can we do about Split Ends?

Though we cannot refrain from injuring our hair, careful grooming of the hair is likely to delay the appearance of 'splits': avoid rubber bands, spiky brushes and combs; avoid combing wet hair. Conditioners protect the hair against physical injury to some extent, so use them regularly. Once splits have appeared, it is a good idea to trim off the straggly ends to give a healthy appearance to the hair.

There is no definite way to mend split ends. Conditioners coat the hair and may temporarily bind splits, making them less obvious. Conditioning the hair with digested gelatin has been found useful.

Chemical Treatment of Hair?

Chemical hair treatments include bleaching, oxidative dyeing, waving and straightening of the hair. The integrity of the hair fibre depends on the presence of bonds between various hair proteins. Chemical treatment of hair results in the breaking of the disulphide bonds, most of which are later reformed. However, even under the best of conditions, ten percent of the broken disulphide bonds are not reformed, resulting in some residual weakness of the hair. So repeated procedures could eventually break the hair.

• • •

43

Dandruff — its Cause and Treatment

Dandruff more scientifically called Seborrheic dermatitis is a disease that causes flaking of the skin. It usually affects the scalp. In adolescents and adults, it is commonly called "dandruff." In babies, it is known as "cradle cap."

Seborrheic dermatitis is a common skin disorder that can be easily treated. Dandruff appears as scaling on the scalp without redness. Seborrhea is oiliness of the skin, especially of the scalp and face, without redness or scaling. Patients with seborrhea may later get seborrheic dermatitis. Seborrheic dermatitis has both redness and scaling.

Know Your Skin

What are the causes of Dandruff ?

The basic underlying disorder is excessive oil production by the skin glands which in turn is acted upon by microorganisms, that might be a fungus, called Pityrosporum ovale. This organism is normally present in the skin in small numbers, but sometimes its numbers increase, resulting in the skin disease.

Dandruff appears as scaling on the scalp without redness. Seborrhea is oiliness of the skin, especially of the scalp and face, without redness or scaling. Patients with seborrhea may later get seborrheic dermatitis. Seborrheic dermatitis has both redness and scaling.

Dandruff causes embarrassment to the patient, in that it manifests clinically as intractable itching and deposition of greasy white scales which are dislocated from the scalp during the process of itching.

Dandruff (Seborrheic Dermatitis) affects the skin of the scalp, face, nose, eyebrows, behind the ears, external ear. Stress, fatigue, extreme weather, oily skin, infrequent shampooing , skin disorders such as Dandruff and use of lotions that contain alcohol may increase the risk of seborrheic dermatitis. Neurologic conditions such as Parkinson's disease, head injury and stroke are also associated with seborrheic dermatitis.

How do we Prevent Dandruff?

There is no way to prevent or cure seborrheic dermatitis. However, it can be effectively treated. The tendency to develop this disorder appears to be inherited. The severity can be lessened by:

- Lessening stress.
- Avoid exposure to extreme weather.
- Use an oil balance formula for an oily skin.

How can Dandruff be Treated?

The treatment of seborrheic dermatitis depends on its location on the body. Treatment also depends on the person's age.

This skin disorder is treatable but may recur. Gentle shampooing with a mild shampoo is helpful for infants with cradle cap. A low strength corticosteroid cream or lotion may also be applied to the affected areas of skin. Adult patients may need to use a medicated shampoo and a stronger corticosteroid preparation. Shampoo the hair vigorously and frequently. Loosen scales with the fingers, scrub for at least 5 minutes and rinse thoroughly.

Nonprescription shampoos containing tar, zinc pyrithione, selenium sulfide, sulfur and/or salicylic acid may be recommended by a dermatologist or a prescription shampoo may be given. However, patients should follow their dermatologist's advice, excessive use of stronger preparations can cause side effects.

More Valuable information about Dandruff...

Dandruff can appear on any part of the skin as patches of varying size. It manifests as white and yellow oily flakes associated with itching. Itching is usually harmless unless there is second degree infection associated. It may cause redness in the area affected with dandruff. Hair loss may also be associated with this disease.

Frequently asked questions about Dandruff...

- Which specialist should I see if I have Dandruff?

  You should see a Dermatologist (skin specialist) and get their opinion.

- Can people who have dandruff use a conditioner?

  Yes, people who have dandruff can use a conditioner to keep up the condition of their hair. A conditioner does not stop the effect of an anti-dandruff shampoo on the scalp.

- Is it true that the more lather produced when shampooing the more effective the shampoo is and the cleaner the hair?

  No, the amount of lather produced has nothing to do with the effectiveness of a shampoo lathering agents are generally added to shampoos because people believe that more lather means cleaner hair and it tells the user where and when to rinse.

- Is it true that the more shampoo you use the cleaner the hair will be?

  No, a small amount of shampoo slightly larger thant he size of a small coin and slightly diluted is usually sufficient for all hair at shoulder length that is washed frequently. The amount of shampoo will vary according to the length of the hair and how frequently it is washed.

• • •

44

Hair Loss and its Treatment

Hair loss is one of the common problems among all of us. All hairs are shed at the end of their growth cycle, so some degree of hair loss is normal. If you have excessive hair loss, it makes sense to first understand the possible causes. There are many possible causes of hair loss, however most hair loss is normal, and part of each person's genetic programme.

The most common type of hair loss is related to both genetic and hormonal make up, and is called androgen-dependent hair loss. About 50% of children with a balding parent of either sex will themselves become bald over a period of time.

Commonly used name for this type of hair loss is male or female pattern baldness:

Male pattern baldness: Is characterized by a receding hairline, and moderate to extensive loss of hair, especially on the crown area.

Female pattern baldness: causes an overall thinning of hair on the head, and a moderate loss of hair on the crown or at the hairline.

What are the causes of Hair Loss?

One of the primary cause of hair loss is a high amount of the male hormone, dihydrotestosterone (DHT) within the hair follicle. DHT is produced from testosterone in the prostate, various adrenal glands, and the scalp. After a period of time, an over abundance of DHT causes the hair follicle to degrade and shortens the active phase of the hair.

Another factor that has been linked to hair loss is the amount of sebum in the scalp. Sebum contains a high amount of DHT, and clogs pores in the scalp, both of which cause the malnutrition of the hair root. The amount of sebum in balding hair is related to the amount of oil in the hair. Meanwhile most doctors agree that frequent shampooing is advised in hair loss cases with oily scalps.

The most important cause of hair loss is inadequate nutrition. Even a partial lack of almost any nutrient may cause hair to fall. But hair grows normally after a liberal intake of these vitamins. A high protein and an iron rich diet is recommended for hair loss. An adequate intake of raw vegetables, fresh fruits, salads, green leafy vegetables should be included in the diet on a regular basis.

Another important cause of falling hair is stress, such as worry, anxiety and sudden shock. Stress leads to a severe tension in the skin of the scalp. This adversely affects the supply of essential nutrition required for the healthy growth of hair.

General debility, caused by severe or long standing illnesses like typhoid, syphilis, chronic cold, influenza and anaemia, also gives rise to hair disorders. It makes the roots of the hair weak, resulting in falling of hair. An unclean condition of the scalp can also cause loss of hair. This weakens the hair roots by blocking the pores with the collected dirt. Heredity is another predisposing factor which may cause hair to fall.

How can Hair Loss be treated?

The healthy condition of the hair depends, to a very large extent, on the intake of sufficient amounts of essential nutrients in the daily diet. Hair is made of keratin, a protein, which also makes up the nails and the outer layer of our skin.

A Well Balanced Diet

Women require 60 grams, men 80 to 90 grams, adolescent boys and girls 80 to 100 grams of protein. It is supplied by milk, buttermilk, yogurt, soyabean, eggs, cheese, meat and fish. A deficiency of some of the B vitamins, of iron, copper and iodine may cause hair disorders like falling of hair and premature greying of hair.

Persons with a tendency to lose their hair should thus take a well balanced diet. An adequate quantity of vegetables seeds, nuts green leafy vegetables, fresh fruits, egg and milk should be included in their diet regularly.

Surgical Hair Restoration

There are many surgical procedures which will help to restore the hair from falling. Surgical restoration is the only permanent solution to baldness. It involves a series of operations that extract plugs of scalp from the sides and back of your head, where hair grows densely, and implant them on top and in front, where you are going bald.

Scalp Reduction

Scalp reduction is performed on patients with well-defined bald spots in the crown area of the scalp. It is sometimes done in conjunction with hair transplantation to reduce the size of the bald scalp, especially in patients who do not have enough donor hair to cover the bald areas.

Tissue Expansion

Silicon bags are inserted beneath an area of hairy scalp and gradually inflated with saline water over a six-week period. This causes the hair-bearing skin to stretch, thus increasing the amount of hair-bearing scalp. After removing the bags, expanded hair bearing skin is lifted and moved to an adjacent bald area where a similar sized patch of scalp has been excised.

• • •

45

Home Remedies and FAQ's About Hairloss

Several home remedies have been found useful in the prevention and treatment of hair loss.

- The most effective among these remedies is a vigorous rubbing of the scalp with the fingers, after washing the hair with cold water. The scalp should be rubbed vigorously till it starts to tingle with heat. This will activate the sebaceous glands and energise the circulation of blood in the affected area, making hair growth healthy.
- Mustard oil, boiled with henna leaves, is useful in promoting healthy growth of hair. About 250 grams of mustard oil should be boiled in a tin basin. A little quantity of henna leaves should be gradually put in this oil till about 60 grams of these leaves are thus burnt in the oil. The oil should then be filtered through a cloth and stored in a bottle. Regular massage of the head with this oil will produce abundant hair.
- Daily application of refined coconut oil mixed with lime water and lime juice on the hair, prevents loss of hair and lengthens it. Application of the juice of green coriander leaves on the head is also considered beneficial.

- Another effective home remedy for loss of hair is the application of coconut milk all over the scalp and massaging it into the hair roots. It will nourish the hair and promote hair growth. Coconut milk is prepared by grinding the coconut shavings and squeezing them well.
- Amla oil, prepared by boiling dry amla pieces in coconut oil, is considered a valuable hair tonic for enriching hair growth. A mixture of equal quantities of fresh amla juice and lime juice used as a shampoo stimulates hair growth and prevents hair loss.
- Regular use of castor oil as a hair oil helps the luxuriant growth of the hair.
- Washing the hair with a paste of cooked black gram dhal, (urad dhal) and fenugreek (methi) lengthens the hair. A fine paste made from pigeon pea or red gram (arhar dhal) can also be applied regularly on bald patches, with beneficial results.
- Certain home remedies have also been found useful in case of patchy loss of hair. The seeds of lime and black pepper seeds, ground to a fine paste, is one of the valuable remedies. This paste applied on the patches, has a mildly irritant action. This increases blood circulation to the affected area and stimulates hair growth. The paste should be applied twice a day for a few weeks.

These home remedies will be definitely effective and useful for preventing hair loss.

Frequently asked questions about Hair Loss...

- Which specialist should I see if I have hair loss?

  You should see a Dermatologist and a General Physician.

- Is stress a factor in hair loss?
  Sometimes stress can play a role in diffuse loss. Stress-induced loss ordinarily regrows within a year of eliminating the cause.
- How long does it take to see results from any treatment programme?

Best results are often seen after the two-year mark. This is because hair follicles undergo a relatively long dormancy period in between growth cycles (usually about 3 months). In addition, hair only grows about inch per month in non-thinning areas and usually considerably slower in thinning areas. Since it generally takes several cycles of growth/fallout/regrowth, with the hair getting thicker and longer each time, it can take a great deal of time to see noticeable improvement. Note that best regrowth results are seen with hair that was lost within the last five years and in areas of the scalp in which there is still some fine hair.

What is DHT?

Dihydrotestosterone, which is produced from testosterone by the enzyme 5-alpha reductase. DHT is the androgen thought to be most responsible for male pattern baldness. DHT has a very high affinity for the androgen receptor and is estimated to be five to ten times more potent than testosterone. Other androgens that may be significant in pattern loss include androstenedione, androstanedione and DHEA (especially in women). All of these fall into hormonal pathways that can potentially result in elevation of DHT downstream via various enzymes. It is possible that certain DHT metabolites may play a role in pattern loss as well.

Word Meaning

Alopecia Areata: Alopecia Areata is the medical term for hairloss which occurs in patches on the scalp.

Androgens: Androgens are often referred to as male hormones.

DHT (Dihydrotestosterone): DHT is a male hormone that is suggested to be the main cause for the miniaturisation of the hair follicle and for hair loss. DHT is formed when the male hormone testosterone interacts with the enzyme 5-alpha reductase.

Baldness: Receding hairline.

Scalp: tissue covering the skull.

Follicle: The hair follicle houses the root of the hair.

Scleroderma: A disease of the skin and connective tissue that can cause hair loss over the affected areas.

Testosterone: A predominantly male hormone which promotes the development of male characteristics.

Keratin: A protein by which hair is made and also makes up the nails and the outer layer of our skin.

• • •

46

Hair Removal by Laser

Are you tired from the rashes and cuts from shaving, or the burns, pain, and ingrown hairs from waxing? Have you ever considered using **hair removal lasers**? There are many benefits for using hair removal lasers, but you should still weight your options carefully and decide if it is right for you. Like with many things, these won't necessarily be as effective for one person as they are for others.

There are two different options for hair removal lasers; however they both rely on heated lights. One of them is called a laser beam, and the other is called an intense pulsed light, often referred to as an IPL. Lasers, as you probably already know, are beams of light that are focused. An intense pulsed light on the other hand involves the use of interspersed flashes. For either of these it usually takes about five monthly visits to rid your-self of about 70% of your hair. It takes this long because your hair grows in cycles and you want to be sure that you kill as much as possible.

Hair removal lasers do not work well on everyone. The best candidates tend to pale skinned people with darker coloured hair, although darker people with lighter coloured hair can also get good results with a couple of extra treatments. Since it is practically impossible to know what results will be the results really just depend on a few things. First of all, you will get better results from better lasers, and then there is of course your skin and hair type. Finally, it also depends on the number of treatments you undergo.

The price of your treatment will completely depend on where you live, the areas you're having treated, and the quality of the laser and facility doing the treatment. It can cost anywhere from $200 to $500 a session, and it takes five or more sessions just to permanently free yourself of about 70 percent of your body's hair. After that, you can get touch-ups for anywhere around $100-$150, again depending on where you are, your hair type, and the quality that you are after.

Now when you think about all of this, you begin to wonder about scarring. This of course also depends on the quality of the hair removal lasers that are used. If you go to a discount place, then you can expect scarring, the more you get done the more scarring there will be. For this reason you want to avoid these places and go to the places that have trained technicians. These will be the medical facilities that are truly established. You will not be offer any kind of discount at these places, however, there is a very good chance that you will have no scarring that you would get at other places. This doesn't mean that you should jump at the first place that works this way, it means that these are the places you should do research at.

• • •

47

Benefits of Laser Skin Care

Over the years, laser hair removal treatment has been accepted and has increased due to a better understanding of their use. Laser hair removal treatment can be the best form of hair removal, but is not for everyone. Contrary to the common concept of laser hair removal is not permanent. During laser hair removal treatments work by producing light at different wavelengths, output and pulse width. Wavelength provides the point of falling into the laser, such as melanin (dark pigment organic), water

or veins. The lasers used for hair removal are designed to burn structures that contain dark pigment. Therefore, laser hair removal treatments work best for people with lighter skin and dark hair. Similar to electrolysis, the hair follicles in the growth phase (Anage) are more easily damaged than those in the resting phase (Taloqan). It should be noted that at least 15% of the time, hair follicles are being Taloqan. That makes it impossible for permanent hair removal, and treatment must be repeated.

Laser **hair removal** treatment uses laser beams to heat the hair follicles and render them inactive. Treatment can affect thousands of hairs, but because hair grows in different stages multiple treatments may be necessary. Laser hair removal only affects hairs that are in the stage of active growth and is therefore a series of treatments may be necessary. Throughout his treatment of laser hair removal, your doctor will press a handheld laser to the skin will be activated for a split second to warm up the follicles. This process has proven to be safe and effective, and many current lasers are equipped with cooling devices to minimize any skin damage that can occur during permanent hair removal. Requirements for laser hair removal is necessary because the process is very technical and has to be done by a medical expert or doctor. Laser hair removal is at risk for certain types of skin. Dark-skinned people are prone to the effects of laser hair removal, which can burn or blisters.

A condition called "bands" is a common occurrence after undergoing laser hair removal and can be a traumatic experience for a first timer. Apart from that there are different types of blond hair, like red hair and did not respond well to laser hair removal. Determine if your skin is ideal for laser hair removal is what we called the hair removal for a prescription. If you have excess hair and decide to do something about it in a permanent level, there is only laser treatment which can achieve the desired results. There are some conditions that the candidate must meet in order to undergo the laser treatment. The type of skin should be examined as well as skin reaction to treatment. A doctor or cosmetic surgeon can do this. Once the doctor determines that the sequels are not worth the bother, since it is only very recently, he or she may issue a prescription hair removal you may not undergo treatment for permanent hair removal. These processes are lengthy and require several sessions over a period of three to ten months depending on the candidate countries.

Laser treatments are performed by a trained technician or nurse, and can last from a quarter of an hour and a half hour. It is a common occurrence for laser treatments to give a feeling uncomfortable for the patient. The discomfort is not a problem when small areas involved, but causes problems when treating larger areas. There are ways to reduce the degree of discomfort. One is to use ice in the area before the laser session. In general, laser hair removal treatments require no pain medication or sedatives. Treatment is relatively easy and did not have much time to recover. Unlike waxing, you can shave before treatment. Sometimes the skin may turn purple, and this condition may last several days. In addition, some areas may be temporarily blisters. If you are interested in Lazer hair removal as a method of permanent hair removal, hair removal Lazer this guide will explain in detail everything you need to know about laser hair removal and treatment of what is at stake. Laser hair removal treatment uses laser light to remove unwanted hair. It involves intense, pulsating beam of light to heat the hair follicle and make it inactive. Multiple treatments may be required prior to permanent hair removal is accomplished, and almost all areas of the body including the upper lip, neck, chest, back, armpits, legs and can be treated.

• • •

48

Rules of Hair Dyeing

What wrinking is to skin, greying is to hair. Both are the signs that herald age. A woman despairs as much over the wrinkles that begin to line her face, as she does over the hair that turns white. This feeling of regret, for the youthful years that have passed is nothing new. In fact, the effort to retard the ageing process has existed since Eve. Beauty treatments, geared to delay or cosmetic world. Ageing, however, is a natural process. With time, the body ages and the signs of ageing manifest themselves in various way... greying is one of them.

To understand the greying process, one must have a basic idea of the structure of the hair. The hair consists of concentric layers. The outermost layer is the cuticle, which is made up of tiny, transparent scales that overlap each other. The second layer is the cortex. It is in the cortex, just below the surface layer, that pigment, darker the colour of the hair will be. With age, pigment may not form, causing hair to be without colour or white. There may be other reasons why pigment may fail to form, but age is the most common factor.

The white strands mix with the dark ones and give the impression of grey hair. Naturally, when white strands appear, the question of how to deal with them causes much concern, not just from the aspect of concealing them, but also checking further greying. This question makes it important that few facts about the hair be known, so that damage to the hair is minimal.

To begin with, the strands that have already turned white cannot become black or dark again. The only way to change their colour is by dyeing. Dyeing, in fact, has become a common practice and a number of women resort to it. Unfortunately, most of them do not know the way the structure of the hair can be affected. Unless this is known, one is not able to take precautionary measures that help to control damage to the hair. Dyeing or colouring hair is not a modern beauty device. Women of ancient Rome and other civilisations were known to dye their hair, or even bleach them, using ingredients that often caused irreparable damage.

The chemical dyes and colourants that are in use today can also harm the texture and health of the hair. They contain ingredients that penetrate the cortex, resulting in damage to the texture. Regular dyeing, therfore, results in hair that is dry, brittle, rough and without lustre.

If hair damage is to be checked, it is essential to setup a protective care routine, as protection itself is one of the best preventive treatments. It has also been seen that regular care, started in good time, not only delays greying, but can also prevent it from spreading. These treatments include the use of products, containing natural hair darkening and protective agents, that have the added capacity of improving and maintaining the health of the hair.

If the decision is made to dye hair with chemical dyes, it is all the more important to treat hair regularly with natural products, in order to protect the hair from harmful effects of chemicals and keep hair damage to the minimum. Dye your hair, if you must, but help to restore its beauty in terms of texture, quality and quantity.

Nature of Hair Dyes

One of the main advantages of using natural hair dyes and colourants is that they are completely safe and subject the hair and scalp to no hazards. Natural vegetable products are non-toxic and do not harm the structure of the hair. They do not destroy the outer layer or cuticle, as they do not enter the cortex. Henna is probably the best known natural colourant. It has the capacity of strengthening hair, as it coats the hair shafts. This not only protects hair, but gives it body and sheen. If there are only a few white strands which are visible there is no necessity to use chemical dyes. Henna can be used very effectively to conceal them.

Coffee or Kaththa (catechu) added to the henna paste gives hair a richer brown colour rather than a reddish tinge. The coloured strands blend with the rest of the dark hair and are well concealed. A question that is commonly asked is whether henna will colour the entire hair a flaming red. The answer to this is very simple. Dark hair will not catch a lighter colour and will not be coloured red. Henna will, in fact, add gloss and brighten dull hair.

Special henna powders, containing other valuable ingredients like amla and khol are available. They have been used very successfully both as protective and preventive treatments, apart from curing many hair disorders. Regular applications of henna will not only conceal but provide many other benefits. If there are a considerable number of strands that have already turned grey and you decide to dye them black, you should have a basic idea of the process that is involved.

Chemical dyes have a toxic base and have been known to cause irritations and allergies. The hairdresser will therfore do a patch test before dyeing your hair. This is usually done by applying the dye on a tiny area just behind the ear. A period of 24 hours must be allowed to see if any skin irritations or allergies are caused. If not, the dye may be used. It is better to have the hair dyed by a hairdresser, as there are particular instructions that must be followed regarding the lotions used and great care must be taken. No attempt should be made to dye eyebrows or eyelashes with these dyes.

Fin hair can be dyed easily as it absorbs better, while coarse hair is more resistant to colour. This itself would require the use of more and more quantities of the dyeing lotion as time goes on, since dyeing makes hair coarse, with repeated applications.

Shampoos

Shampoo, rinse, tonics and conditioning powders, containing ingredients like henna, amla, shikakai, reetha and 'brahmi' have proved successful in maintaining the hair texture and health. These ingredients also have specific curative properties.

As far as the daily routine is concerned, the hair should be washed with a very mild shampoo is ideal, as not to subject it to harsh detergents. An amla shampoo is ideal, as it lubricates dry hair and has a powerful cleansing action without disturbing the oil moisture balance. It also restores the acid-alkaline balance of the scalp. Amla keeps the hair soft and shiny and checks further greying. The harsh ingredients in chemical dyes remove natural oil and moisture, leaving both the hair and scalp very dry. A hair rinse, used with shampoo, completes the hair washing procedure and leaves hair in manageable condition.

Regular conditioning treatments with henna improves both the look and the general health of the hair. Thus hair that is dyed requires special care, so that the damage may be reversed to a great extent.

One of the most important aspects of beauty is to be aware of the detrimental effects of various treatments. Some treatments can have disastrous results, involving a great deal of time, effort and expense to gain what is lost. In some cases, damage may be permanent. As far as possible, avoid treatments that expose the hair and skin to harm. For instance, when you feel you must resort to such methods, be sure to supplement them with an appropriate routine of daily care, so that the natural beauty of such valuable assest may be preserved as long as possible.

• • •

49

Diet for Skin and Hair

Your skin is a true reflection of your inner health. Anything wrong inside is bound to show outside.

Diet for Skin

A well-planned menu comprising a sensible and well balanced diet ranks foremost in the skin-care regime. To realise the impact of the diet on skin, it is important to be informed on what the inadequancies and deficiencies in diet can bring on us.

Deficiency	Consequence
• Vitamin A	Thickening of skin of texture Wrinkles Aggravation of acne
• Vitamin B Complex	Skin pallor Pigmentation Dark circles under eyes
• Vitamin C	Acne problem Uneven lightening of skin colour
• Vitamin E	Pigmentation
• Proteins	Loss of skin rejuvenation. Degeneration of connective tissue Under neath the skin surface.

• Minerals-	
Zinc, Calcium and Iron	Skin pallor Spot discolouration
• Oil and Moisture	Excessive skin dryness and chapping.

There is no one particular food that can singularly provide all the essential ingredients for your health. A well balanced diet comprises a host of different kinds foods. Bear in mind that each food item in assortment is rich in one or two of the essential ingredients.

To help you design a menu, both tasteful and healthy, here's a list of various food items and the nutrition value they bear. An assortment of these items can truly make a gourmet meal.

- **Vitamin A**

  Fish liver oil

  Butter

  Liver

- **Carotene**

  Carrots

  Leafy vegetables

  Red and yellow sweet potatoes

- **Vitamin B**

  Whole wheat

  Pulses

  Rice (parboiled, home-pounded)

- **Vitamin C**

  Orange, Lemon

  Leafy vegetables

  Guava

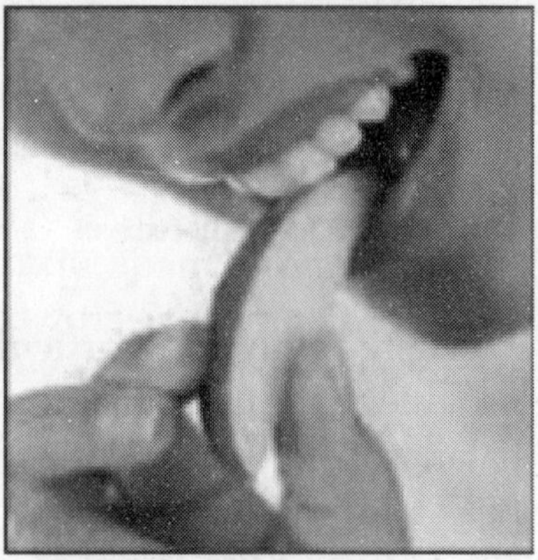

- **Vitamin D**

  Fish liver oil

  Egg yolk

  Butter
- **Vitamin E**

  Sunflower oil

  Palm oil

  Margarine
- **Vitamin K**

  Cabbage, spinach

  Lettuce

  Beef liver
- **Proteins**

  Soyabeans, Meat, Fish

  Skimmed cow's milk

  Beans and Peas
- **Calcium**

  Cheese - Hard and Soft

  Milk - Cow's (fresh)

  Various nuts
- **Iron**

  Liver, Eggs

  Pulses

  Green leafy vegetables (Raw)

Diet for Hair

A nutritious diet is essential for our growth, well–being and long life. The same is true for the hair. Since hair is the least important of all the human organs, it gets the minimum nutrition from the blood that which is left-over after the needs of the vital organs–the hearts, lungs and liver. Therefore hair displays the first signs of nutritional deficiency of the body when it occurs.

Hair is an extension of your skin and is composed of cells that have rinse from generative cells deeper within the body–cells which are formed, some four to six weeks earlier.

Since hair is made up of protein called keratin hair needs protein for its growth and well–being. Now here are some super protein food items apart from meat, that are good for your hair. Scientists have come up with a way of assessing which protein foods are better than others. Their frame of reference is termed "biological value" and the basic is the amount of food required to meet human needs.

Eggs: Have the largest amino acid methionine than any other complete protein. In addition, eggs contain large quantities of Vitamins A, B, D and E and many minerals including sulphur. One egg a day can give a real boost to your hair.

Milk: Milk is not just for kids, it's for everyone. It is a complete protein with built-in extra vitamins and minerals that spell lovely hair. All adults should have one glass of milk a day-plus one serving of paneer (cottage cheese), ice cream or Dahi.

Yoghurt (Dahi): is the oldest health food. It contains lactic acid and possesses all the nutrients and proteins in a form which can be easily assimilated by most people. Dahi has large amounts of Vitamin B Complex along with bacteria which aids digestion and elimination.

It is suggested that those on antibiotics should have a cup of Dahi every day an antibiotics kill the useful bacteria which our hair and skin need.

Sunflower seeds: is low in calories and a good source of complete protein, high in poly-unsaturated fatty acids and rich in vitamins and minerals.

Vitamins: If you are eating well, it should not be necessary to take vitamin or mineral supplements. Vitamins A, D, E and K can cause liver damage if taken in excess. The B group of vitamins, however, are water-soluble and the body will take up only what it requires. Vitamin B is essential for healthy skin and hair and has been considered "food for the nerves" as well as being used to relieve some forms of pre-menstrual tension. So a daily dose of yeast tablets is useful.

Yeast: The composition of a yeast cell is very similar to the composition of the cells that make up the human body. It is a tremendous source of protein and Vitamin B.

Hair Enemies: Acturally, the enemies of your hair are also the enemies of your health. When planning your diet, remember that much of what we eat contains toxins and toxic substances. This does not mean that they contain certain ingredients that the body does not need or cannot use. These have to be removed from the body, and the organs through which they are excreted include the liver, kidneys, bowel, lungs and sweat glands. Too many toxins can overwork these organs, causing ill-health, early signs of which could be in the case of the hair and scalp, reduced hair growth, excessive oiliness or dandruff.

A diet high in snack foods, potato chips, cakes, pastries, white bread, foods with high level carbohydrates, sugar-laden soft drinks containing refined sugar or artificial sweeteners or preservative, flavouring and colour, fizzy drinks and fake orange and lemon juice. Factory farmed meats and vegetables can also be high in toxins although these are often difficult to avoid when shopping at the local super-market.

• • •

50

Homoeopathic Remedies for Various Skin Disorders

Homoeopathy is based on symptiom˘Similarity.

Shingles

Use a homoeopathic treatment only in the absence of other significant health problems. If there are other significant health problems, consult your physician. One dose of the selected medicine should be given every 12 hours in 30 potency and should be stopped after any reaction is noted.

Arsenicum Album

Useful when the eruption burns intensely and there is relief in warmth but aggravation from cold air and cold applications.

Rhus Tox

Use when there is intense itching and pain, the appearance of small blisters filled with a watery, yellow fluid and there is a lot of discomfort and restlessness at night.

Lachesis

Use this if the rash is dark red or has a purplish hue and the eruption is painful and sensitive when touched and is worse on the left side of the body.

Ranunculus bulbosus

Use when there is an attack of shingles involving the back and chest, and severe pain, especially in the ribs, which is worsened by touch, motion or lying on the rash as well as sudden exposure to heat or cold.

Mezereum

May be used when there are burning or sharp pains even after the eruption has gone. Patients are often chilly and sensitive to touch and cold.

Iris Versicolor

Especially useful if the rash has affected the right side of the abdominal and chest region, and where there is the appearance of small blisters with dark points. The patient may have digestive upsets.

Other medicines for this condition include Apis, Mercurius, Hepar sulph and Sulphur.

Warts

As this is a constitutional imbalance, it would be a very good idea to seek professional help.

Some Useful Homoeopathic Remedies

Causticum

May help with moist and jagged fleshy warts, especially on the fingernails or on the face and warts with extra growth on them.

Dulcamara

May help in large, flat warts, especially prevalent on the backs of hands, fingers and on the face.

Antimonium Crudum

For hard, horny and smooth surfaced warts, especially on the hands.

Nitric acid

For warts on the face and lips. The warts may be soft, irregular and accompanied by sharp pains and bleeding. It is advisable to see your doctor with this type of wart.

Ringworm/Athlete's Foot

Choose a suitable remedy according to symptoms and administer a single dose once a day for three days. If the symptoms improve change, stop the medicine and allow recovery to take place.

Sepia

Most useful for simple ringworm infections where there are circular, scaly patches, usually brown or reddish-brown. There may be itching and burning.

Tellurium

Use when the ringworm is more red than brown, with prominent rings. Small, itchy blisters releasing a thin liquid may appear on the rings.

Graphites

Use when there is a significant thick, honey-coloured discharge and the scales are thick.

Arsenicum

May help very dry ringworm with rough scales, a burning sensation and a discharge of clear lilquid on scratching the area.

Note: For ringworm of the scalp, all the above medicines are helpful.

Candida (Yeast Infections)

If this is a recurrent problem, seek professional advice. Choose from the list below according to the most appropriate symptoms. Take twice daily for two to three days and stop when symptoms change.

Bellaldonna

Use when the skin is bright red and swollen with inflammation.

Chamomilla

For nappy rash with irritability.

Graphites

For a honey-coloured discharge, and when raw areas become encruster. The skin may, however, appear just dry, rough and cracked.

Hepar Sulph

Use when there is a secondary bacterial infection and pimples and pus form on raw areas which smell unpleasant. There will be extreme tenderness of the inflamed parts.

Thrush

When there are thrush infections of the mouth, the following remedies are suggested.

Borax

The best remedy to try initially if symptoms do not indicate otherwise. There may be sores on the mucous membrances, dryness in the mouth, a little swelling and bleeding.

Mercurius

Use when the mouth is sore and inflamed and emits an unpleasant odour; there is considerable salivation, the gums are soft and bleed easily and may be streaked with white lines; the tongue is puffy and coated, either with a black, white or dirty - yellow colour.

Hydrastis

For a large amount of thick mucus in the mouth and on the tongue, which experiences a burning sensation.

Eczema

This is a chronic and deep-seated condition, and so consultation with a skilled homoeopathic practitioner is strongly advised to determine individual diagnosis and remedies.

Hives

If this is recurrent, seek professional advice.

Some Useful Homoeopathic Remedies

Apis

The most likely medicine for the condition, where the hives are intensely itchy and aggravated by warmth, and may come out during perspiration and after exercise. The remedy is particularly helpful for hives which cause swelling around the eyes, and when hives look swollen and waterlogged.

Urtica Urens (stinging nettle)

This may be considered when the symptoms are similar to those needing Apis and are especially prevalent after strenuous exercise.

Rhus Tox

Use this if the condition seems to be caused by rubbing, scratching or wetness, and is much worse at night, causing restlessness.

Kali Bichromicum

Use this for chronic acne.

Sulphur

Use this for inflamed and infected pustules.

Psorinum

Use this for itchy infections.

Bruises

Arnica Oil: Rubbing this on to the affected area may be helpful.

Arnica cream or ointment

Use this only if the skin is unbroken. It is better to take Arnica internally if it is broken.

Sprains

Use ointment Rhus Tox and keep the organ wrapped.

• • •

51

Indian Henna — A Herb for Hair

Henna is a Persian word, which describes a small flowering shrub (Lawsonia inermis). It is found all over the world, including India, Pakistan, Morocco, Yemen, Iran, Afghanistan, Somalia, Sudan, Libya, Egypt and Bangladesh. However, the variety of henna plant varies from region to region. Different plants have different colouring properties and hence, the colour of the powder also varies. Henna has been used for thousands of years, for its medicinal properties and cosmetic properties. Apart from this, it is also used for colouring and conditioning the hair and in the form of body art.

Henna powder, in its pure and natural form, is a bright or deep green, khaki or brown. The colour produced by pure natural henna ranges from orange to red, to black cherry and near black colour. Contrary to the popular belief, pure black colour is not produced by natural henna powder. Talking about its production, henna powder is made from the leaves of the henna bushes. When manufactured in large quantities, the leaves are taken to the factory and machine grounded. Normally, henna powder is made by blending different types of henna leaves from different parts of a country or from different countries.

Once the leaves have been grounded, the powder is sifted. This is because, if not sifted, the henna powder will contain pieces of the leaves. The finely sifted henna powder contains no leaves, making it best for cosmetic use. Henna powder colours the skin, when the dye is released, as a result of the henna powder being mixed with water or lemon juice and being applied on the skin. Henna, when applied to the body parts such as hands, arms, legs, near the naval region and at the back, is called mehndi. For a simple mehndi design, it may take about 10 to 15 minutes, but if you want to go for an intricate design, you might need to invest several hours.

After application of henna, you need to dab it, with a lemon-sugar solution when it becomes firm on the skin. This is essentially done to preserve the paste. Unlike tattooing and piercing, henna does not hurt, because it is applied on the surface of the skin with an applicator and not injected into the skin. Traditionally, a cone is used for making the designs. However, mehndi can also be made using a bottle, with a fine silver nozzle tip. People enjoy the cooling sensation felt after the application of mehndi. This aromatic mixture, apart from conditioning the skin, gives a natural soothing effect.

Henna has, today, become a part of all major festivals and celebration. Be it, Purim, Eid, Diwali, Karva Chauth, Passover, Nowruz or Mawlid, it has graced every occassion with its presence. Celebrations like wedding, birth of a baby and birthdays seem to be incomplete without the ceremony of henna. Brides, in the present time, typically have the most complex patterns of henna, to express their greatest joy and wishes for luck. With an improved technology being used for its cultivation, henna available today, has an enhanced dye content and greater artistic potential than earlier.

• • •

52

Herbs and Home Remedies for Various Skin Disorders

Herbs for Hair

From organic foods to herb based cosmetics, the cycle has turned a full circle, back to nature. Synthetic shampoos are now accused of causing several irritations, including dandruff and excessive dryness of hair and scalp. Now the natural goodness and purity of nature's gift to beautify hair and skin have been rediscovered. More and more women, all over the world are realising the real worth of natural herbs for cosmetic purpose. Vegetable dyes and rinses were already known in ancient times. But these have come back into fashion in the past two years. Synthetic conditioners, tints, rinses and dyes deprive the scalp of nature oils and proteins.

Herbs are being used to bring life to dull hair, to colour grey hair, and to bring a change in the original colour of the hair and also to clean it.

Rinses like Camomile tea is claimed to give a golden tint to hair, which Chinese tea is supposed to brighten dark hair.

Dyes: Herbs like henna, walnut bark, indigo, which were used even in the ancient times when women first started being conscious of beautifying their hair and skin are still in practice.

Indigo: Gives a blue colour to the hair. It is mixed with henna to make what is called the Persian dye, still widely used in the East. The colour obtained varies according to the proportion of the two ingredients. It must be left on the hair for several hours for the dye to be effective.

Walnut Bark: Gives an attractive brown colour to the hair. Henna is the Persian name for a small shrub. A paste made of powdered henna leaves is of ancient repute as a cosmetic. It has been used by Egyptian and Indian women to dye their finger nails and make intricate patterns on their hands and feet in an orange red colour, which was considered to add to their beauty.

It was and is still used for dyeing hair and beards, as well as horses manes. Moreover, distilled water from the flowers is used as perfume too.

Henna is used by beauticians to get a bright red colour or a burnished copper, or just to get highlights. Henna gives a coppery bronze or reddish effect. Mixed with coffee seeds, the hair assumes a rich brown colour.

Henna when used on grey hair gives a carroty red colour; used on dark hair, it gives a rich auburn tone. Henna is usually applied on strands of clean, shampooed hair while it is still damp and is left on the hair for an hour or so.

Hair, your crowning glory, needs thorough cleansing and gentle care. Synthetic shampoos have been accused of leaving the hair "squeaky"-which means they wash off the natural oils from the hair. Herbs like reetha, shikakai, amla have retained their popularity and are used by many to keep hair clean. But to overcome the messy, tedious process of using these herbs, a new brand of herbal shampoos have been introduced. These herbal shampoos claim to be 93 per cent pure, made from herbs procured in India and abroad. These are obtained in four different varieties, to suit four kinds of hair, namely Orange Blossom for oily hair, Camomile for dry hair, Wild Cherry for normal hair and Rosemary for dandruff. The shampoos are made from the softest water and pure extract of fresh cured herbs in a floral, oily and cherry base.

• • •

53

Juice Therapy for Allergy and Hair Loss

Allergy

An allergy is a reaction to a substance that in nonsensitive persons would produce no effect. It is an antibody- antigen reaction that may be caused by the release of histamine or histamine-like substances from injured cells. The offending substance is known as an allergen and can be anything that brings on the symptoms of an allergy.

General Recommendations

Food allergies should be identified, and problem foods should be avoided. Blood tests are more effective than the skin scratch test in identifying food allergies. Certain additives, such as aspartame (Nutra Sweet), monosodium. glutamate (MSG), and sulfites, can also cause allergic reactions. In addition, an overgrowth of the yeast known as Candida albicans can cause a variety of food sensitivities. Either a blood test or stool culture can determine whether there is a yeast overgrowth present in the body. When this yeast overgrowth is brought under control, many people notice that their allergies and sensitivities have improved. In addition, the Juice has been helpful for many allergy sufferers.

Nutrients That Help

- Vitamin B6 may be beneficial for MSG sensitivity.
- Vitamin B12 may have therapeutic benefits. Speak to your doctor about supplementation, as this nutrient cannot be obtained from juices.
- Vitamin C may reduce blood histamine levels and MSG sensitivity.
- Vitamin E has antihistamine activity.
- Molybdenum may be helpful, as this nutrient might be deficient in the majority of people with sulfite sensitivity.
- Lactobacillus acidophilus and Lactobacillus bifidus, may be beneficial, as a deficiency may exist with food allergies. Speak to your doctor about supplementation, as these substances are not found in juices.
- Bloflavonolds potentiate the action of Vitamin C.

Beneficial Juices

- Kale, spinach, and sweet pepper–Sources of Vitamin B6.
- Kale, parsley, and collared greens–sources of Vitamin C.
- Spinach., asparagus, and carrot–sources of vitamin E.
- Cauliflower.
- Orange, cantaloupe, and parsley–sources of bioflavonolds..

Dietary Modifications

- Identify food allergies and eliminate those foods that cause symptoms.
- Avoid additives that commonly cause reactions, including MSG, softies, and aspartame (Nutraf-tleet).

Suggested Juicing Recipes For Allergies

Vitamin E-Rich Drink

Small handful spinach	Bunch up spinach and push
4-5 carrots, greens removed	through hopper with carrots
3-4 asparagus spears	and asparagus.

Cherie's Cleansing Cocktail

½-inch slice ginger root	Push ginger, beet and apple
1 beet	through hopper with carrots.
1/12 apple, seeded	
4 carrots, greens removed	

Molybdenum Drink

Small handful spinach	Bunch up spinach with garlic
1 garlic clove	and push through hopper
4-5 carrots, greens removed	with carrots and cauliflower.
4 small cauliflower buds	

Hair Loss (Alopecia)

Alopecia is natural or abnormal baldness or thinning of the hair. It can appear in patches or over the entire head. Hair loss can result from the aging process, surgery, radiation, severe illness, drugs, endocrine disorders such as hypothyroidism, sudden loss of weight, vitamin or mineral deficiency (especially iron), overconsumption of supplements such as Vitamin A and Niacin, poor diet, stress, certain forms of dermatitis. pregnancy, and hereditary factors. There are over a dozen types of alopecia. Therefore, if you suddenly lose large amounts of hair, it may be appropriate to consult your physician to rule out any underlying medical problem that may be causing this loss. Be aware, though, that it is normal to lose about forty to eighty hairs per day.

General Recommendations

Some people lose hair after an illness because of an accumulation of oils, dead cells. and medication residues at the hair follicle. These residues can "choke" the hair, causing it to fall out. Ask your beautician or beauty supply store about products that remove such residues from hair and scalp. A rinse of sage tea or apple cider vinegar can help hair grow, as can a scalp massage with ginger root juice tonic or with a tonic that combines cayenne pepper with vodka. Lying on a slant board for fifteen to twenty minutes per day will cause blood to flow to the scalp and daily scalp massages will also help improve circulation. To encourage hair growth, make an infusion with the herbs horsetail, catnip and southernwood and use as a rinse. Use only natural hair products; avoid using harsh chemical products on your hair.

Stimulating hair growth from within by the foods you eat is even more important than what you put on your scalp and hair. Vitamins, minerals, amino acids, and other nutrients provide the raw materials from which hair is produced. Our American diet is too rich in foods that actually "starve" the hair, subh as fat, sugar and refined foods. You may need to make certain dietary modifications to encourage your hair to grow.

Dietary Modifications

- Include plenty foods rich in the sulfur-containing amino acids L-cysteine and Z-methionine, which are found in animal products (eggs are an especially rich source), legumes and cabbage. Skin, hair and nails contain some of the body's most rigid proteins, all of which have a high sulfur content. Eat animal proteins in moderation, however an ample serving of lean meat, poultry or fish is three to five ounces, depending upon your body size. Eastern medicine says that eating too much meat can cause hair loss.

- Cut down on sweets. Eastern medicine also says that too much sugar-especially fruit sugar (fructose)--can cause balding on the sides of the forehead. It is found that sugar is often a contributing factor in hair loss, and that after sugar is certain individuals, the hair-loss removed from the diets of certain individuals, the hair-loss process is either halted or totally or partially reversed.
- Include foods rich in the D vitamins, with special emphasis on choline, inositol and PABA. Choline is plentiful in eggs, wheat gram, legumes (beans, split peas, and lentils), oatmeal and brown rice. Lecithin, wheat germ, rice bran, whole wheat, and legumes are excellent sources of inositol PABA is found in mushrooms, cabbage, sunflower seeds, wheat gram, oats, spinach, and eggs.
- Make sure that your diet contains ample essential JattV acids. Eat fish two or three times a week (not deep-fried). If your hair is dry and brittle, you may improve its texture by supplementing your diet with expeller-pressed flaxseed oil, keep it only in refrigerated opaque bottles.

Nutrients That Help

- B-complex vitamins are essential for health and growth of hair.
- Vitamin C helps improve circulation to the scalp.
- Vitamin E improves hair health and enhances hair growth

Beneficial Juices

- Green leafy vegetables–sources of B-complex vitamins.

- Kale, parsley, green pepper, and broccoli–sources of vitamin C.
- Spinach, asparagus and carrot–sources of vitamin E.
- Alfalfa-helps to stimulate hair growth.
- Ginger juice-used traditionally to stimulate circulation to the scalp.

Suggested Juicing Recipes for Hair Loss

Very Special

1/2 handful parsley
Handful watercress
4 carrots, greens removed
3 stalks celery
½ cup chopped fennel
½ apple. seeded

parsley, and watercress, and push through hopper with carrots, celery, fennel. and apple.

Hair-Growth Special

2 dark green lettuce leaves
Handful alfalfa sprouts
4-5 carrots, greens removed

Bunch up lettuce and alfallfa. and push through hopper with carrots.

Ginger Carrot Special

1/4-inch slice ginger root
4-5 carrots, greens removed
1/2 apple, seeded

Push ginger through hopper with carrots and apple.

Potassium Broth

Handful parsley
Handful spinach
4-5 carrots, greens removed
2 stalks celery

Bunch up parsley and spinach leaves, and push through hopper with carrots and celery.

Green Special

1 large kale leaf
2-3 green apples. seeded
Lime twist for garnish

Bunch up kale leaf and push through hopper with apples. Garnish with lime twist. Vie surprise is that you won't taste the kale!

Hair Growth Tonics

Ginger Juice Tonic

1- to 2-inch piece ginger root

Juice ginger root. Pour the juice on your head and massage into the scalp. Let dry for 10-15 minutes; then shampoo. Ginger rootjuice has been used naturopathically to stimulate circulation to the scalp. Your head will feel a tingling sensation, as if it just had a Certs!

Cayenne Pepper Tonic

4 oz. red cayenne pepper

I pint 100-proof vodka

Mix red cayenne pepper with vodka. Let sit for two weeks, shaking the mixture several times. Then strain until the liquid is pepper free. (A nylon stocking works well for straining.) This makes liquid capsicum pepper. (It is is not for drinkingi) Each day, apply this mixture to thinning or bald areas of the scalp. Within five or six weeks hair should begin to grow. This may not work for hereditary baldness.

• • •

54

Ayurvedic Medicines for Skin and Hair

Skin is not only the outer covering of the body but it is a sense an excretary organ also. The glow of skin shows our good health.Here are some ayurvedic medicines.

Skin Cracked

- For dry, cracked hands apply a mixture of grated potato soaked in olive oil. Leave this on for 10 minutes and then rinse off.

For Face

Pound a piece of radish to a pulp and just apply this pulp on the face. Keep it till it is dry. Then rub it off by cold water. Internally, consume radish, its juice and the radish vegetable cooked by steam heat. It is better to leave salt altogether till your blood is clean. The acne results because of impurity of blood.

- Mix 1 teaspoon lemon juice in 1 teaspoon finely grind cinnamon (dalchini) powder and apply on affected areas frequently. Sift the cinnamon (dalchini) powder to make it into a very fine powder.
- Crush a few garlic (lahasun) flakes and apply on the face, once or twice a day. Swallowing 1-2 flakes of raw garlic regularly helps further.

- Grind some neem leaves with water to a fine paste. Apply on infected area.
- Make a paste of 1/2 teaspoon each of sandalwood and turmeric (haldi) powder in little water and apply.
- Grind some black cumin seeds (Jeera) with a little vinegar (sirka) to a smooth paste. Apply on affected parts.
- Clean face with cotton wool dipped in rose water 2-3 times a day. Do not use soap.
- Orange peel is very good in the treatment of acne. Grind the peel with some water to a paste and apply on affected parts. When oranges are not in season, you may use a powder of dried orange peels. For this, when oranges are in season, dry orange peels in shade. Powder finely in a grinder and sift it to make it a very fine powder. Store in an air tight bottle for future use.

Blackheads

- Mix 1 teaspoon lime juice in 1 teaspoon finely grind cinnamon (dalchini) powder and apply on affected areas frequently.
- Mix 1 teaspoon each turmeric (haldi) powder and juice of fresh coriander (dhania) leaves and apply daily on a face before going to sleep.

Pimples

- Grind equal quantity of nutmeg (jaiphal), black pepper (kali mirch) and sandalwood. Apply on affected area.
- Clean face with rose water (gulab) 2-3 times a day.
- The orange peel (santre ka chilka) is very valuable in the treatment of acne and pimples. Pound the peel with water on a piece of stone and apply on the

affected area. When oranges are not in season, dry peels in the shade. Powder the dried peels. Sift to get a fine powder and store.

- Rub nutmeg (jaiphal) in unboiled milk to form a paste. Apply on the face and let it dry. Wash it off with warm water. Do it 2-3 times a day. You will see the pimples disappearing in 3-4 days.
- A couple of garlic (lahasun) cloves crushed and rubbed on the face 1-2 times a day. This process is further helped by taking raw garlic regularly. Have 1-2 cloves in the morning.
- Apply fresh lemon juice on the affected area overnight. Wash off with warm water next morning.
- Grind some neem leaves with water to a fine paste. Apply on infected area.
- Application of fresh mint (pudina) juice over face every night cures pimples and prevents dryness of the skin.
- Mix equal amounts of lemon juice and rose water (gulab jal). Apply on face and keep for ½ an hour. 15-20 days of this application helps cure pimples and also removes blemishes and scars.

Scars on Face

- Wash face with coconut water (nariyal pani). Apply coconut water on face and leave for 15-20 minutes before washing it off.
- Grind one teaspoon yellow mustard (peeli rai) to a paste with 1 tablespoon malai/cream and apply on face and neck. Leave for 15-20 minutes. This also removes itching as well as blemishes from the skin.
- Wash and grind a few fresh mint (pudina) leaves to a smooth paste. Apply and leave for 1/2 an hour or

apply every night before going to sleep. This helps in getting rid of pimples along with the blemishes.

- Apply a teaspoon of olive oil mixed with 1/2 teaspoon of lime juice, leave it for 20-25 minutes and then wash off.
- Take the pulp of a ripe tomato. Add a few drops of lemon juice and rub on the face and neck. Leave for 20-25 minutes before washing.
- If your skin is dry, rub a stick of sandalwood in milk and if skin is oily, rub it in rose water (gulab jal) and then apply on face. Leave for an hour and then wash with cold water. This is very effective during summers.
- For a dry and blemished skin, mix a tablespoon gram flour (besan), add a pinch of turmeric (haldi), 1/4 teaspoon orange peel (or santre ka chilka) powder, a teaspoon curd (dahi) and a teaspoon of milk. Apply on face and neck. When skin feels taunt, rub it off with finger tips, and wash off wih tap water.

Scars Due to Burn

- Boil 1 cup neem bark in 4 cups water. Remove from fire and shake liquid. Apply the emerging froth on the affected area. Repeat several times and for several days.
- Blanch and grind a few almonds to a fine paste with 2 tablespoons milk and one tablespoon each of orange and carrot juice. Apply well on the face and neck. Leave for 1/2 an hour, then wash off.
- Apply one tablespoon finely grind raw papaya on face and neck. Keep for 15-20 minutes and wash off.

Pustules

- Take half kg turmeric powder and boil it and add about 200 gms. of pure honey to it. Keep the mixture as it is for two weeks in a glass jar. Now strain it and fill in a clean bottle. Take 10 to 15 gms. of this Aasav (mixture) after food. This will cleanse your blood of the impurities which cause pustules. Also dip a cotton piece in turmeric oil and place it over pustules for relief.

To Open Shrinked Pores of the Skin

- Mix one tablespoon tomato juice and a few drops of lemon juice. Apply on open pores. Wash after 15-20 minutes.
- Rub a cube of ice everyday, on the area where open pores are present. Wash face with cold water. Never use hot water on face.

Face-Freckles (Jhanyin)

- These are mainly caused by using creams and lotions indiscriminately which burn the outer layer of the skin. Take just 10 gms. of grind turmeric and drench it in the milk of the banyan, peepal or aak tree. Make a thick and uniform paste of it in the evening and cover it with a lid. Keep it as it is overnight. Massag your face with this ubtan at least half an hour before you take your bath. Continue this treatment for a week to remove all the freckles. Then use ubtan just once a week.

The Decoction or Karha

- Decoction made out of chukander or beetroot leaves is very effective to cure this trouble. You can prepare the karha in the following manner:
- Take a few pieces of beetroot (chukander) and dice them to small pieces. Boil them in water when they become tender, crush them as much as to reduce them to a pulp. Again add a little water and boil the whole lot once again. When you find the solution becoming homogeneous and thick, cool it and strain it through

a coarse cloth or strainer. The karha is ready. Wash your hands and feet with this karha everyday when you retire for the day. It is always better to keep your hands and feet immersed in this diluted karha before washing them with the water. In about a couple of days your skin will become soft and glowing. This karha would be used for application on the dry face.

Skin Allergies

- Grind 1 tablespoon poppy seeds (khuskhus) with 1 teaspoon water. Add 1 teaspoon lime juice. Apply on the affected areas.
- Mix 1 teaspoon lime juice with sandalwood paste and apply all over.

Skin Irritation

- Take clean water and rub vigorously a piece of cucumber to make its thick paste. Then apply the paste on the skin for its cure in two three days time. But the patient should not consume heat producing items like spicy food, tea and even lots of common salt.

Itching

- Extract juice of tulsi and massage on the parts of the body itching. If the trouble be chronic, take about 2 parts of tulsi juice and one part of til oil. Allow them to boil on slow fire. Then cool it and put it in a bottle. This is most effective oil for all sorts of itching problems.

Ring worms

- Take a large piece of pure turmeric and gently rub it over a stone slab (sil) drenched with water. Take out the rubbed portion of turmeric from the stone slab and apply the paste over the rings on your body.

When the paste dries apply another layer of the turmeric paste over it. In a couple of days time the trouble will start to end and the sprouts will also disappear. Don't discontinue the treatment once you get well. It is better to apply the paste for a week more for total relief.

Eczema

- Add 1 teaspoon camphor (kapoor) to 1 teaspoon sandalwood paste and apply on the affected areas.
- Mix a paste of turmeric (haldi) and neem leaves (1:1) in a little gingelly oil (til ka tel) and apply on affected areas.
- Grind 1 tablespoon each turmeric (haldi), neem leaves and gingelly oil (til ka tel) into a fine paste and apply on the affected parts.
- Rub a nutmeg (jaiphal) against a smooth stone slab with a little water and make a paste. Apply on affected parts.
- Stop using any soap and wash your body with neem soap.
- Grind pure sulphur and add in pure mustard oil and apply on your body.
- Take about 6 gms. of soda bicarb and pour in the juice of half a lemon over it. Add about 20 gms. of mustard oil and massage your body vigorously with this mixture. Then take sun-bath for about 2 hours before you go to take your bath. It is especially effective if your skin is dry.
- Extract the juice of leaves of beetroot and mixing it with honey, Apply it over the affected part. In about a week's time this trouble will end.
- Apply freshly pounded radish pulp over the affected part. Allow it to dry. In about half an hour take bath

in hot water in which some perfume is added. In about a week's treatment the affliction shall be removed.

Warts

- Mash the garlic (lahasun) cloves and apply externally.
- Apply the milky juice exuding from the stems of figs (anjeer) and leaves on the affected areas.
- Place some chopped onions in a dish. Cover with salt and leave overnight. Twice a day apply the resulting juice to the warts until they disappear.
- Another alternative is fresh pineapple juice or slices. Since pineapple contains an enzyme that breaks-down warts, it is very effective in removing warts without leaving behind any marks. Apply some to the warts several times in a day until it has gone.

Sunburn

- Mix 2 teaspoons tomato juice and 4 tablespoons buttermilk (chhach). Apply it. Wash after 1/2 an hour.

Mix olive oil with equal quantity of vinegar and apply an hour before your bath.

Sweating Excessive

- Mix dry sandalwood powder in rose water (gulab jal) (1:1) and apply over parts where sweating is excessive.

Thorn

- If a thorn has gone in your child's foot and is not coming out, simply mix jaggery (gur) and carom seeds (ajwain) and tie on it. The thorn will come out on it's own.

Wrinkles

- Apply coconut oil on the portions of skin and face where wrinkles set in and gently massage every night at bed time.
- Soak shredded ginger (adrak) in honey. Eat a spoonful every morning.

Body Dry Itch

- Grind 1 tablespoon poppy seeds (khuskhus) with 1 teaspoon water. Add 1 teaspoon lime juice. Apply on the affected areas.

Body Heat

- Add 2 to 3 drops of almond oil to pomegranate (anaar) juice and drink.
- Remove seeds from fresh amla fruits and grind the pulp into a fine paste. Tie it in a muslin cloth and squeeze out the juice. Take 2 teaspoons of this juice and mix it with two teaspoonfuls each honey and lime juice. Add 1 cup water and drink on an empty stomach every morning.
- Take a tender bel fruit. Grind it with 1 cup milk. Apply on the head and massage well before taking a shower.
- Soak 8 to 10 almonds and 1 teaspoon rice overnight. Remove the outer skin. Grind into a fine paste. Mix with some milk and add a pinch of turmeric powder (haldi) and sugar candy (mishri) to taste. Boil and drink.

Burns by Fire

- Immediately apply glycerine on the burnt area.
- Burn a handful of mango leaves to ashes and apply this on the affected parts.

Burns by Hot Water

- Take the thin bugs of banana leaves. Bandage directly on affected areas. Tie the upper part for two days and then lower parts for two more days.

Palms, Burning Sensation

- Grind a handful of bitter gourd (karela) leaves into a smooth paste and apply on the affected areas of feet and palms frequently.
- Finely grind a handful of henna (mehendi) leaves and add 2 tablespoon lime juice. Stir and apply on the feet.
- Apply finely grated bottle gourd (lauki) on the feet.
- Mash 1 ripe banana along with a little curd and water, take twice a day.
- Grind a handful of bitter gourd (karela) leaves into a smooth paste and apply on the affected areas of feet and palms frequently.

Heat Exhaustion

- Apply some sandalwood oil on the forehead.

Heat Stroke

- Have the cooling drink 'panna'. To prepare this, cook unripe or green mangoes in hot ashes. Extract the pulp and mix with water and sugar. You may even pressure cook the mangoes if you cannot make provision for the ashes.

Prickly Heat

- Mix dry sandalwood powder with rose water (Gulab jal) to make a paste. Apply on affected parts. When dry, wash it off. It prevents excessive sweating and heals inflammed skin.

Burns, Scar

- Boil 1 cup neem bark (neem ki khal) in 4 cups water. Remove from fire and shake liquid. Apply the emerging froth on the affected area. Repeat several times and for several days.

Burns on Body

- Apply curry leaves (kari patta) as poultices over affected areas.
- Spread a thin layer of honey over the burn and cover with a dressing. Repeat this regularly every two or three hours till it heals.
- Mash a ripe banana and apply on burns. Bandage with betel leaves (pan ka patta).
- If you have a minor burn, immediately place an ice pack on the burnt area for 10 minutes.
- Combine 4 teaspoons each of lime juice coconut oil and rub until the mixture turns white. Apply on affected parts.

Cracked Feet/Soles

- Finely grind a handful of heena (mehendi) leaves. Add 2 tablespoons lemon juice and apply on the feet.
- Mix the juice of bottle gourd (lauki) and sesame oil (til ka tel) in the ratio 4:1 and heat till the moisture has evaporated. Bottle and use over cracked skin.
- Mix equal quantities of glyceine and lemon juice. Apply every night before going to bed. This mixture can be made and stored in a glass bottle.
- Massage your feet with castor oil every night (in winters) for 2-3 minutes and then wear socks at night.
- Grind equal amounts of neem leaves and turmeric (haldi). Apply on affected area.

Feet Smelling Bad

- Soak feet in strong tea for 20 minutes everyday until the smell disappears. To prepare your footbath, dip two tea bogs in 500 ml of water for 15 minute and pour the tea into a basin containing two litres (10 cups) of cool water.

Unpleasant Body Odour

- Soak 10-15 basil leaves in 1 cup water and eat every morning for a month.

  Grind neem (azadiracta indica) leaves and apply in armpits and on other parts of body.

Black Spots

- These may be caused by excessive indulgence in the sexual pleasures which sap your vitality and these black spots appear. Extract a little juice of tulsi and add two times more lime juice. Make their homogeneous solution and apply this solution or paste over these spots every night with soft hands. The spots will be removed in a week's time.

Boils

- Slightly roast big onion on a naked flame. Mash it and mix in a teaspoon each turmeric powder and ghee. Apply and tie a bandage.
- Mash the garlic (lahasun) cloves and apply externally.
- Grind neem leaves into a paste and apply on affected parts.
- Apply a paste of ginger (adrak) powder and turmeric (haldi) 1:1) on boils.
- Grind some black cumin seeds (kala jeera) in a little water and apply the paste on the affected areas.

- Heat black pepper powder in 1/2 teaspoon ghee untill charred. Use this as an ointment.
- Take fenugreek leaf (mehi patta) paste, heat it and when lukewarm, apply on the affected part of the body.
- Soak bread in warm milk and sandwich the mixture in between the folds of a clean cotton cloth. Apply this Poultice to the boil and hold in place with a cotton bandage.This draws the dirt to the surface of the skin and simultaneously bursts the boil.

Hair Falling

- Take a handful of neem leaves and boil them in 2 cups of water. After cooling and filtering, use the decoction for rinsing hair.

Baldness

- Collect the soft and green leaves of beetroot and boil a few in water. When the leaves become tender and soft take them out of the water. Now grind the leaves fully to a homogeneous pulp. If water is needed, only that water should be used in which the leaves had been boiled.
- Repeat the procedure in a similar way but this time replacing the beetroot leaves with henna. Now grind both the leaves together. Apply this paste over the head liberally. Allow it to dry and then wash it with lukewarm water in which a few drops of lime juice have been added. Repeat the process for one full month. It is expected that within this period hair will again start to sprout on the bald area. After doing this treatment for one full month, repeat it after every week. It is a very good remedy and many bald people have now lush growth of hair. But, as told earlier, it

could be useful only when the baldness has not been due to the hereditary factor.

- Rub on the scalp 1 teaspoon oil in which raw mangoes have been preserved for over one year. Repeat this treatment frequently.
- Grind 1 tablespoon liquorice root pieces (mulathi) in 1 cup milk with 1/4 teaspoon saffron (kesar). Apply this paste on bald patches at bedtime continuously.
- Grind fenugreek seeds (methi daana), with water and apply on the head. Leave for at least 10 minutes before washing. Do it every morning for a month.
- Boil 1 cup mustard oil (sarson ka tel) with 4 tablespoon henna (mehendi) leaves. Filter and bottle. (Massage on the bald patches regularly.)
- Grind the remains of tobacco smoked in a hookah and add to boiling mustard oil. Cool and store. Massage on the bald patches regularly.

Hair Greying

- Wet a lemon half and rub lemon juice into the scalp well.Wash off after it runs dry.
- Grind 1 tablespoon each, pulp of amla and lime juice. Massage this into the hair before going to bed. Wash it next morning.
- Soak shredded ginger (adrak) in honey. Eat a spoonful every morning.

Hair Thinning

- Bathe the hair in 1 cup coconut milk twice or thrice a week for a few months.

Dandruff

- Put about 21 leaves of tulsi and 10 gms. of Aanwala Churna in a big bowl. Add a little of water to make a paste of them. Apply it evenly on your head and allow it to dry. Then wash it with cold water. This will prevent hair loss and clear dandruff also.

- Mix equal quantities of dried curry leaves (curry patta) lime peel (nimbu ka chilka) . Shikakai, fenugreek seeds (methi daana and green gram moong saboot) and grind them finely. Store and use as a substitute for soap or shampoo.
- Apply fenugreek (methi) seeds, grind with some water and paste it on the head. Allow to soak at least for 40 minutes before washing. Use every morning for a month.
- Soak 2 tablespoon fenugreek seeds (methi daana) in water overnight. In the morning grind into a fine paste. Apply all over scalp and leave for 1/2 an hour. Wash with Shikakai or mild shampoo.
- Boil a handful of neem leaves in 4 teacups of water. After cooling and filtering use for rinsing hair.

Lice

- Grind the seeds of neem into a fine powder and mix in some groundnut oil. Apply to the scalp. Allow it to remain overnight. Wash off next morning.
- Mix 1 teaspoon lime juice with 1 teaspoon garlic (lahasun) paste and apply on the head.
- Grind 7 to 8 almond (badam) kernels with 1 to 2 teaspoons lime juice and apply on the hair.

55

Tips for Nail Care

Nail care is important when it comes to personal grooming. Suppose a woman has applied makeup carefully and attired herself with most fashionable clothes, but has been careless about her nails. How do you think she would look like then? Won't it be a bit shabby? It happens in our everyday life. Indeed it would be better if we give some more attention to nail care. Here are some essential tips on nail care which would definitely help you a lot.

Nail Care

- Take care of your nails between salon visits.
- File your nails regularly and always keep them short.
- If your nails are exposed to chemicals, moisture, water, etc, it could result in split peeling nails or allergic reaction. Wear rubber gloves to protect your nails or coat them with some cotton.
- Never use something like scissors for both for infected and non-infected nails.

Artificial Nails

- Always get artifical nails applied by a good technician.
- Artificial nails would need manicure or refilling every two or three weeks.
- If you decide to remove them, appropriate solution is not difficult. Even when the artificial nails are removed, natural nails remain in the same condition.

Nail Tip Design

- Using glue could damage your nails, even if it is applied on polish layers.
- Ensure the last polish layer is dry before applying the next. Use layers of different colours.
- Keep on experimenting with nail tip design. You could use Chinese characters, apply small fake tattoos or create different patterns.
- You could use band-aids for applying design. Cut band-aids and stick them on top of a dry coat of polish. Contrasting colour would look good.

For Acryllic Nails

- Keep your acrylic nail polished. Thick polish could cause bubbles and uneven application. So first add a drop of polish and then dilute it thinner.
- Before applying any acrylic layer, clean your nails. If the nails have remnants of cuticle oil, old polish or lotion, the new polish would not apply itself properly.
- For avoiding bubbles, remove the excess from the brush along the bottle's border.
- Lay a base coat to protect your nails and in the process, help helps the acrylic layer to stick in proper way.
- Use a nail stick to clean up the acrylic on the skin around the fingernail.
- Seal the polish with a top coat to camouflage possible bubbles or streaks.
- Seal the polish with a top coat to camouflage possible streaks or bubbles. It also adds shine.
- Allow enough time to the nails to dry.

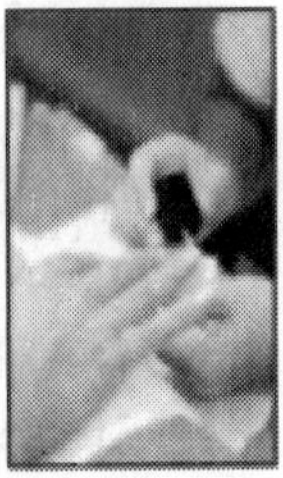

56

Nail Manicure

Your nails need to be taken care of too. Giving your nails a manicure is a good way to take care of them and pamper them. Given below are the steps to achieve the perfect manicure at home.

- To begin with remove all traces of your nail polish. Use as many cotton balls as needed.
- Use a nail file or an emery board to shape your nails. File in one direction only. Do not use the seesaw motion. To shorten the nail, use the course side of the emery board first and finish with the finely textured side.
- Work on your nails carefully and with respect. Do not go overboard with your manicure.
- To check if your nails are well done run your nails over a pair of old pantyhose. Your nails should not snag the hose.
- Apply cuticle remover cream and gently push back the cuticles using a cotton bud. Never cut your cuticles. Massage away dead skin using circular movements.
- Apply hand lotion and massage your palm of your hand with the thumb of your other hand. This will

improve blood circulation. Work your way all over your hand and repeat with your other hand.

- Before you paint your nails, clean them with an orange stick that has been wrapped with cotton and dipped in nail polish remover and rub over the surface of the nail. Remove any creamy residue, if there is none then you can polish your nails.
- While polishing your nails being in the centre of your nail. Paint one stroke down the centre and then the sides of the nail. You should paint a nail in three strokes. Let it dry completely before applying the second coat.
- Apply colour after your nails are completely dry. Use a base coat before applying nail polish. Then apply a colour of your choice and do not apply a new coat before the previous one dries. You should apply three coats of colour. After applying colour apply topcoat and it will give added protection and help your nail colour to last longer without chipping.
- Store nail polish in the fridge. To prevent the cap from sticking apply a little vaseline around it.

• • •

57

Foot Care Routine

When it comes to beauty care one aspect of our body that we tend to neglect often is our feet. Your feet carry the weight of your entire body and if often one of the most abused and least cared for parts of your body. Foot care is very important in order to keep your feet healthy and beautiful. The skin on your feet is very delicate and foot skin care on a regular basis is a must if your feet are to look beautiful. Given below is a foot care routine, that is simple and is not time consuming and that you can follow a few times a week.

- The first step to good foot care is to remove the hard skin from your feet. You may have to use a pumice stone or apply cream generously on the area in order to remove the dead foot skin. Soak your feet in a bowl of slightly hot water. This will soften the dirt and the dead skin, which will allow you to remove it easily. You could use a foot file as well, rub your skin gently and rinse off the flaky residue.
- After this soak your feet for about 10 min in a bowl of warm water. Add some mineral salts or palm sea salts, along with a few drops of lavender essential oils that will relieve the aches and reduce the swelling.